VALIDITY ISSUES

IN

EVALUATIVE

RESEARCH

Edited by

Ilene N. Bernstein

SAGE PUBLICATIONS · *Beverly Hills / London* · 1976

H
62
.V27
1979

The material in this publication originally appeared as a special issue of SOCIOLOGICAL METHODS & RESEARCH (Volume 4, Number 1, August 1975). The Publisher would like to acknowledge the assistance of the special issue editor, Ilene N. Bernstein, in making this edition possible.

For information address:

SAGE PUBLICATIONS, INC.
275 South Beverly Drive
Beverly Hills, California 90212

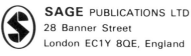

SAGE PUBLICATIONS LTD
28 Banner Street
London EC1Y 8QE, England

Printed in the United States of America

International Standard Book Number 0-8039-0581-5

Library of Congress Catalog Card No. 75-32373

THIRD PRINTING

CONTENTS

VALIDITY ISSUES
IN
EVALUATIVE RESEARCH

VALIDITY ISSUES IN
EVALUATIVE RESEARCH
An Overview

*e*valuation research, as a form of social policy research, is expected to provide reliable and valid information useful for policy makers who operate in the world of action. This mandate necessitates a variety of research strategies and considerations not ordinarily pertinent to more basic discipline research. Moreover, the political setting in which evaluation research is conducted demands special attention to the fit between methodological techniques and the research problem. It is to these problems of fit that we address ourselves here.

Coleman (1972) suggested a set of principles for executing social policy research and a set of characteristics that distinguish it from discipline research. The major differences are (1) definition of primary audience, (2) interest in, and formulation of, the research problem, (3) definition of guidelines for the mode of dissemination, and (4) criteria by which to judge research quality and research utility. For policy research, the world of action defines the rules; the scientific community does so for discipline research. It is the differences in values and priorities between these two groups that precipitate many of the problems that make evaluation so complex.

Coleman's specification of principles, along with recent compendiums of evaluation research literature (e.g., Caro, 1971; Rossi and Williams, 1972; Riecken and Boruch, 1974; Struening and Guttentag, 1975) and empirical reviews of evaluation studies (e.g., Wholey, 1970; Stromsdorfer, 1972; Bernstein and Freeman, 1975), all show that the central problem is, as expected, the research design. For our purposes, what is important is that the political demands for certain types of information require multiple and varied design strategies, and the political problems that affect the implementation of particular design strategies require the use of analytic procedures that can provide some corrections for defects resulting from the use of less than optimal designs.

While all procedures need to fit the demands of the research problem, in evaluation research certain aspects become particularly problematic for purposes of design and data analysis. These include (1) specification of the research question(s) to be addressed; (2) selection of the appropriate population to test the hypotheses; (3) selection, assignment, and maintenance of subjects in treatment categories; (4) designation of a system that provides for early estimates of immediate program effects; later, more conclusive estimates of intermediate effects; and estimates of long-range effects; and (5) selection of data sources and/or analytic procedures that can serve as correctives for defective design strategies arising from constraints on the research.

THE RESEARCH QUESTION

In discipline research, one begins with a dependent variable and hypothesizes about factors that would predict that variable. To deduce hypothesized relationships, one examines theoretical statements about the phenomenon of interest. In evaluation research, the procedure is often reversed. One begins with an independent variable—the program—and is asked to assess how it affects a set of only vaguely identified goals. This reversal presents a variety of demands. First, one needs to learn from persons in the world of action (e.g., policy makers, persons administering the action program, legislators interested in the program and/or the problem it is aimed at) what the "specific" goals are. (Anderson, 1975, discusses the consequences of a lack of a priori specification of the dependent variables of interest.) Second, since the research results are ultimately used in the world of action, it is best to elicit specific expectations about the nature of the hypothesized relationships. That is, it is necessary to determine the levels of changes in the goal measures that will be policy relevant apart from whether such changes are more or less than statistically significant. Third, one needs to treat as problematic what the treatment is, or what the program inputs are. It is necessary, thus, to identify the program inputs, to assess the degree to which persons administering the treatments agree with that common definition of inputs, and to assess the degree to which the treatment is implemented for the target population in accordance with the definitions. The Head Start evaluation, among others, testifies to the consequences when these points are ignored. Furthermore, Bernstein and Freeman (1975) found that 22% of the 236 evaluations they reviewed took no measures of program implementation; clearly, then, prospective evaluation researchers still need to be reminded of these considerations.

SELECTION OF THE APPROPRIATE POPULATION

Assuming one has satisfactorily specified the research questions, and specified the dependent and independent variables on which data will be collected, the next task is to determine the appropriate target population and corresponding sample. In discipline research, the sample is normally defined according to its appropriateness for testing the hypothesized relationships. However, as noted, in evaluation research the research question often follows from, rather than precedes, the problem of interest. Thus, the sample cannot be selected. It has already been defined by virtue of its relationship to the program being evaluated. Accordingly, the task is not to determine an appropriate sample, but rather to determine how the available sample can best be used and supplemented so as to rule out potential threats to internal and external validity.

Primarily, the problem stems from the fact that the target population defined for most social action programs is rarely representative of any larger population; furthermore, the target population often manifests characteristics that can be obvious threats to validity. For example, first, in terms of internal validity, statistical regression occurs when persons have been selected on the basis of extreme scores; however, in evaluation settings, persons on the far ends of the continuums of poverty, mental illness, deviant behavior, and the like, are commonly the target populations. Second, differential selection of persons into the experimental program and/or differential selection-maturation interaction may provide a rival hypothesis to a finding that the social action program precipitated the desired outcome; however, in evaluation settings, persons are often initially selected into the sample on the basis of such factors as their willingness and desire to participate in the program. Furthermore, we have reason to believe that, for persons with the same social problems, those who participate can be distinguished from those who do not on maturational factors. Third, subject attrition, i.e., experimental mortality, poses a threat to internal validity. Because this is such a common and severe problem, we address it here in a separate section on maintenance of subjects. Summarily, the implication of the above for a research strategy is that we need to assess ahead of time the areas in which an available sample violates necessary assumptions (e.g., equivalent rates of maturation) and to build corrective techniques into the research design. Anderson (1975), Alwin and Sullivan (1975), and Porter and Chibucos (1975) address such problems.

In terms of external validity, Bernstein et al. (1975) specify five problem areas for evaluation research: (1) selection effects, (2) measurement effects, (3) confounded treatment effects, (4) situational effects, and (5) effects due to differential mortality. As stated, these issues become problematic because the target population in the catchment areas of the social program is, more often than not, nonrepresentative of the larger population to which one needs ultimately to generalize. Insensitive to problems of generalization, experimental social action programs (especially demonstration programs) are often designed to capitalize on the unique, be it a country setting for a drug program, a charismatic leader for a self-help alcoholic retraining program, or a job funding program for ex-convicts initiated by a mayoral candidate campaigning for office. Anderson (1975), too, reviews the problems that ensue from utilization of designs that fail to control for such administrative-type variables.

While many threats to external validity could theoretically be dealt with by drawing comparisons to control and/or matched comparison groups, the number of variables that must be controlled necessitates far too many comparison groups, given the budgetary allotments for most evaluation studies. Thus, once again, the researcher must determine ahead of time, by experience and by careful review of evaluations done of similar programs, the major biases that are likely to threaten generalizability, and then must build corrective devices into the research design.

One final problem related to the delimitation of an appropriate sample needs to be noted, i.e., the determination of sample size. In part, because of a recognition of the disadvantages of having evaluators "inherit" a sample, recent large-scale experiments have been funded where greater flexibility was given the evaluator to select appropriate samples. However, the experience in the negative income tax experiments has shown that what is an appropriate sample to test some hypothesized relationships is not necessarily appropriate for others. For example, the use of the Watts-Conlisk optimum allocation model has made obvious two problems.

First, it fails to consider the optimum allocation for all dependent variables of interest. Thus, as discussed in Lyall (1975) and Anderson (1975), one is often left with sample sizes so small that, in the face of large error variance, one cannot detect changes on the dependent variables. Second, and not unrelated, is the fact that when one uses the optimum allocation model, it is assumed that one knows a priori what all the dependent variables of interest are. However, as was noted earlier, this is often not the case in evaluation research. Furthermore, even when care has been taken to anticipate this problem, still some policy persons will inevitably ask well after the research has been conducted: "Well, if the program doesn't affect Y_1, how about Y_2, Y_3, and Y_4?"

SELECTION, ASSIGNMENT, AND MAINTENANCE OF SUBJECTS

The evaluation research literature is replete with rationales for using approximations to, rather than true, experiments. However, according to Boruch (1974), each of the arguments regarding feasibility, scope, utility, and ethicality can be shown to be at least somewhat overstated. Moreover, Boruch (1975) not only provides counterarguments, but has elsewhere compiled and presented as well an extensive list of examples wherein experiments have been mounted. Thus, our contention is that true experiments can be implemented, especially if one makes use of instances of natural randomization, experiments within quasi-experiments, and the like (see Boruch, 1975, for further discussion). In such cases, random assignment of cases should not be problematic.

The above notwithstanding, the assignment of persons to treatment and control groups is often deemed problematic for still another group for which one might argue alternatives are available. That is, often evaluation researchers approach the design issue as if the only way to conceive of a strategy is the dichotomous arrangement of one treatment group and one control group. Furthermore, they mistakenly assume that control necessarily means the total absence of stimuli. If we recall that policy makers are interested first in ameliorating some social problem, and second in assessing the degree to which some program affects that problem, then we can recognize the logic of assigning persons to multiple groups, each of which experiences a different set of inputs as a variation of the experimental treatment. By assessing the effects of these various combinations of inputs, we not only gain insight into the treatment's general potential for effectiveness, but we also learn what set of inputs (which variety of treatment) maximizes benefits and minimizes cost. Such a design strategy also eliminates the need to convince various persons that withholding services from the needy is necessary to scientific research. Finally, such a strategy also allows us to anticipate such questions as "What effect could the program have if we altered it in this manner?"

Again, the above notwithstanding, there are real instances in which the basis for assignment of cases to treatment groups, even to varied treatment groups, is problematic. In social experiments that have been highly publicized in advance of case assignments, and in which cases persons recognize or suspect that assignment to one variety of treatment will be more beneficial than assignment to another, problems are likely to occur. Anderson (1975) discusses this matter in connection with the Gary Income Maintenance Experiment. We suggest that prospective researchers recognize the potential existence of such difficulties and build into their design budget and plan the cost of measures that will enable them to induce persons to participate in spite of assignment to treatments perceived by such persons as having no personal advantages. However, because even cash payments do not ensure participation, we also recommend that various forms of inducement be pretested in a pilot study before commencing a large-scale effort where such inducement will be essential for the successful implementation of the experiment.

One frequently occurring consequence of ignoring this potential problem is differential attrition of subjects during the course of the research effort. Bernstein et al. (1975) discuss this occurrence in relation to external validity. Similarly, Anderson (1975) notes sample mortality as a serious problem for large-scale experiments. Clearly, if an evaluation is to assess the effectiveness of some program in precipitating a desired change, and if attrition is likely to be a problem, then we need to build into our research design some method by which to assess differences between those who complete the program totally, partially, and not at all. Furthermore, we need to recognize that despite efforts to induce sustained participation, factors that motivate participation may interact with the treatment variables to produce biased estimates of change on the desired outcome measures. Accordingly, we recommend that data be collected for those who are selected to participate and do so, those selected who do not accept, those who enter but drop out in the initial stages, those who complete part of the treatment, and those who remain throughout. By so doing, one should be able to gain information on the degree to which attrition interacts with the treatment, and perhaps, too, some idea as to the set of variables that predict program attrition. Since no program with a high attrition rate can be considered successful, data that help to predict attrition can be extremely useful to persons in the world of action.

MULTIPLE POINTS OF ASSESSMENT

The above considerations relate to the need to fit or adapt traditional methodological procedures to policy research problems. The need for multiple points of assessing results and reporting is different. Not only is it rare in discipline research, but the norms of the scientific community strongly preclude it. Parsons (1951: 335), Kornhauser (1962: 52-53), and others have asserted that scientists prefer long periods of research time in order to conduct lengthy exhaustive probes, especially when they believe that the results of their research may have practical consequences. Since evaluation research is conducted for the very purpose of "having applied consequences," there can be no doubt that the preference of researchers is to present results that they have had optimal time to test and retest. However, this preference is antithetical to the needs of persons in the world of action. Accordingly, some compromise needs to be reached.

We suggest that prospective evaluators not opt (as have many of their predecessors) for ignoring the demand for early partial results. Rather, they should design research so as to be able to meet the demands of a multiple reporting schedule. The evaluation by Hyman et al. (1962; see also the reference to this work in Bernstein et al., 1975) can be cited as an example: early measures immediately following program participation were used to provide tentative estimates of immediate effects. Shortly thereafter, measures were again taken to test the reliability of the early estimates and to estimate intermediate effects. At several later points in time, measures were again taken to refine the early estimates and the intermediate estimates and to estimate long-range effects. In addition, for later years, comparisons were made between groups that had experienced a similar program, but in varied settings; this comparison permitted estimation of biases resulting from interaction of the situation with the treatment. The advantage of using such a "patched-up design" is that, over time, the researcher can strengthen the reliability of his or her findings and simultaneously can meet the special needs of policy makers.

ALTERNATIVE AND CORRECTIVE DEVICES
FOR DEFECTIVE DESIGNS

Under optimum conditions, one can plan and execute a design that takes care of all the considerations noted above. However, evaluation research is almost never executed under optimum conditions. Thus, even the most sophisticated, experienced, and insightful researchers may find themselves required by circumstances to implement a less than ideal research design. As such, we need to concern ourselves with corrective techniques that will decrease the damage done by the use of defective designs.

Unfortunately, the literature is more bountiful with documentation and case examples of the "defective" rather than the "corrective." Thus, in part, it is to this task that subsequent papers are addressed. The intent is to present a series of papers that explicate methodological problems particularly germane to evaluation research, such that prospective researchers can attune themselves to potential problems. Furthermore, the intent is to present discussions that critically examine a variety of techniques that can be used to increase the validity of research results in spite of defects in research design. While all of the papers have been referenced, a brief summary now of each should serve to end this introduction and to begin their presentation.

The first paper by Anderson focuses on some of the major problems that occur in the process of conducting large-scale experiments, such as cash transfer experiments. Anderson addresses questions of sampling, subject attrition, specification of treatment, and the consequences of not including administrative variables in one's design for the purpose of drawing policy relevant inferences from one's research. Insofar as Anderson points out some pitfalls of experimental designs, presented next is a paper by Boruch that advocates the use of true experiments and true experiments coupled with approximations rather than approximations alone, assuming that a specified variety of conditions are present. Additionally, Boruch presents a set of specific design strategies for coupling aspects of true experiments with quasi-experiments to maximize the desired information. Shifting the focus back to pitfalls, the paper by Lyall examines in detail the consequences of using an optimum allocation model for sampling in large-scale experiments. Following Lyall's paper is Alwin and Sullivan's work which argues for the use of analysis of covariance procedures when random assignment has not occurred. Additionally, Alwin and Sullivan address alternative corrective techniques (e.g., gain scores) and demonstrate why their formulation of the argument supports the use of ANCOVA above all others. While the Porter and Chibucos (1975) paper does not appear here (it was accepted prior to the decision to assemble this special issue), it should be recalled as a good companion piece to Alwin and Sullivan. The final paper by Bernstein,

Bohrnstedt, and Borgatta is a codification of problems of external validity in evaluation research. While some of the factors they discuss are referenced elsewhere, their paper is important because it brings together and organizes an extensive list of factors that threaten generalizability. The concern here has deliberately been limited to methodological issues. It is hoped that these papers will be both useful to prospective evaluators and an important contribution to the developing art of evaluation research.

Ilene N. Bernstein
Indiana University

REFERENCES

ALWIN, D. and M. J. SULLIVAN (1975) "Issues of design and analysis in evaluation research." Soc. Methods and Research 4, 1 (August).

ANDERSON, A. (1975) "Policy experiments: selected analytic issues." Soc. Methods and Research 4, 1 (August).

BERNSTEIN, I. N., G. W. BOHRNSTEDT, and E. F. BORGATTA (1975) "External validity and evaluation research: a codification of problems." Soc. Methods and Research 4, 1 (August).

BERNSTEIN, I. N. and H. E. FREEMAN (1975) Academic and Entrepreneurial Research: The Consequences of Diversity in Federal Evaluation Studies. New York: Russell Sage.

BORUCH, R. (1975) "On ostensible exclusivity of randomized experiments and approximations to experiments." Soc. Methods and Research 4, 1 (August).

——— (1974) Paper delivered to the American Sociological Association Methodology Conference, Loyola University, Chicago.

CAMPBELL, D. T. and J. C. STANLEY (1963) Experimental and Quasi-Experimental Designs for Research. Chicago: Rand McNally.

CARO, F. [ed.] (1971) Readings in Evaluative Research. New York: Russell Sage.

COLEMAN, J. (1972) "Problems of conceptualization and measurement in studying policy impact." Virgin Islands: Social Science Research Council. (mimeo)

HYMAN, H., C. WRIGHT, and T. HOPKINS (1962) Applications of Methods of Evaluation: Four Studies of the Encampment for Citizenship. Berkeley: Univ. of California Press.

KORNHAUSER, W. (1962) Scientists in Industry: Conflict and Accommodation. Berkeley: Univ. of California Press.

LYALL, K. (1975) "Some observations on design issues in large-scale social experiments." Soc. Methods and Research 4, 1 (August).

PARSONS, T. (1951) "The institutionalization of scientific investigation," pp. 335-345 in T. Parsons, The Social System. New York: Free Press.

PORTER, A. C. and T. CHIBUCOS (1975) "Common problems of design and analysis in evaluative research." Soc. Methods and Research 3: 235-257.
REICKEN, H. W. and R. F. BORUCH (1975) Social Experimentation. New York: Academic Press.
ROSSI, P. H. and W. WILLIAMS (1972) Evaluating Social Problems: Theory, Practice, and Politics. New York: Seminar Press.
STROMSDORFER, E. W. (1972) "Review and synthesis of cost effectiveness studies of vocational and technical education." Ohio: ERIC Clearinghouse on Vocational and Technical Education.
STRUENING, E. and M. GUTTENTAG [eds.] (1975) Handbook on Evaluation Research. Beverly Hills: Sage.
WHOLEY, J. et al. (1970) Federal Evaluation Policy. Washington, D.C.: Urban Institute.

Policy experiments represent a powerful tool for testing the consequences of contemplated social programs. However, experimentation in the policy field raises perplexing problems and issues, some of which are not commonly encountered in the literature of experimental social science. This paper examines several issues that seem particularly important and intriguing, drawing heavily on experiences in income maintenance experimentation, one of the largest efforts in policy experimentation to date.

POLICY EXPERIMENTS

Selected Analytic Issues

ANDY B. ANDERSON

University of Massachusetts

*t*he ideal of a controlled experiment has long been recognized as a goal worth pursuing in the social and behavioral sciences for the same obvious reason that made this mode of inquiry the predominant research strategy of the natural and physical sciences: the controlled experiment permits the most unequivocal assessment of a variable's influence on another variable. No other method is as powerful for ruling out competing explanations of observed effects. Furthermore, the gain is usually accompanied by increased precision and economy as well. For these reasons, policy research receives from many quarters the suggestion to pursue its questions with the classical experimental method, controlling physically or statistically those variables known to influence the outcome variable of interest, manipulating the policy variable or variables under consideration, and randomly assigning cases to the policy conditions as statistical insurance against the possibility that other variables might influence the dependent variable being studied. Of course, the problems which accompany attempts to do experimentation in the social sciences are similarly present in policy research. For example, often the charge is

AUTHOR'S NOTE: *This paper draws heavily on the author's experience as co-principal investigator of the Gary Income Maintenance Experiment, which he has worked in since approximately halfway through the three-year project.*

made that social experimentation is artificial, and therefore intrinsically misleading. Other frequently heard objections concern the ability to identify and manipulate the relevant variables and the problems of keeping an experiment free from the effects introduced by having the experiment take place in an ongoing social system full of its own random and nonrandom shocks and influences. There are others.

ARTIFICIALITY

Policy research must contend with all of these problems. However, in some respects, policy research stands in relatively good stead with respect to its ability to deal with these and related issues. For example, the problem of artificiality is to some extent lessened in a project in which participants are actually put under the policy conditions, the effect of which researchers want to assess. Still, Hawthorne effects must be contended with, and shortened time horizons can introduce problems. But again, there are known strategies for incorporating these concerns into the research design. Generally, the defense against the charge of artificiality is strong when respondents really live under the proposed policy program. This is particularly so in comparison to experimental studies in which persons are assigned to groups created by the experimenter and are asked to react to or give opinions about experimentally manipulated hypothetical social situations.

KNOWLEDGE OF RELEVANT VARIABLES

On the issue of knowing and manipulating the relevant variables, again, policy experiments appear to be at least as well off as traditional social research in most cases, and better off in many. To know what variables are important in a given study usually requires that the research questions have previously been studied. While any specific policy experiment may not have this advantage, experience suggests that for social problems resulting in large-scale ameliorating experiments, the problem must have been before the public eye for some time. And, as such, usually there will have been other less drastic, less expensive research efforts aimed at describing or documenting the problem, and perhaps at evaluating the success or failure of intervention programs. Such work can provide researchers with useful information about the relevant variables and how they ought to be measured. Furthermore, control over the policy variables may not be problematic insofar as contemplation of an experimental policy program implies the capacity to institute, on some scale, variations of the nominated policies.

EXTERNAL CONTAMINATION

The problem of contamination from ongoing social and historical events is not so easily handled. Experiments in health care delivery are going to be affected by changes in medicare legislation; income maintenance experiments are going to be affected by changes in the minimum wage or in state welfare laws governing the control group; supported work experiments will be influenced by increases in unemployment; and experimental programs in drug rehabilitation can be affected by changes in the medical and pharmaceutical technology for treatment. The examples can be extended indefinitely, all of which points to the conclusion that the social and historical context serves to make untenable the standard assumption of ceteris paribus (all other things being equal). Furthermore, the longer a policy experiment runs (and to overcome problems of artificiality due to limited duration, it is typically necessary to run experiments for a fairly long time), the more likely it becomes that one or more extraneous influences will have some impact on the dependent variables in policy experiments. However, against this eventuality, several things can be said.

First, while not certain, it is likely that external events sufficiently important to be able to confound an experiment will be known. That is, the researcher will be aware that they are present. And, if that is the case, statistical models are available that can incorporate these events into the model as explanatory variables. Ordinarily, the result is something short of the case in which the events either do not occur, or in cases in which the occurrence can itself be experimentally manipulated; but, ordinarily, something better than simply ignoring the events entirely can be done. For example, economic models often include dummy variables for seasonality, for technological change points, and for historical events of large significance. Or, with spline models, knots may be placed at the points of critical events, thus permitting the response function to have different forms before and after the event. There are other techniques that may be used, all of which share the general feature of permitting the researcher to incorporate, in some fashion, information about an unscheduled, potentially contaminating event, such that some assessment of its influence can be made, partial though the assessment may be.

Second, for some purposes the contamination might be less serious than first thought would suggest. Frequently, there is no a priori reason for thinking that the extraneous factors should influence the control group any differently than they do the experimental group. In this case, although external validity may be compromised, the internal validity, i.e., the correct assessment of control-experimental differences, need not be impaired, unless some sort of interaction effect between the event and the treatment levels is presumed to exist. Moreover, the problem of external validity is not necessarily lethal because generalization can always be qualified to hold only for situations comparable to those under which the experiment was conducted. For example, an income maintenance experiment might report findings for a time period during which a large strike was in force, separately from the findings for the rest of the experiment. Or a health facility utilization experiment might separately analyze data from before and after the institution of a large mass transit system presumed to have affected utilization. While potential confounding remains, it is unreasonable to assume that the data lose all utility because every conceivable alternative explanation cannot be ruled out. Moreover, for some extraneous factors, there is a net gain in the utility of the experimental findings insofar as the extraneous factors may well be events that can be presumed to occur in the world to which the researcher wishes to generalize. To illustrate, it is important to know how mass transit changes might affect facility utilization, or how labor disputes and strikes will affect income maintenance programs. The fact that these events were not planned and manipulated may prevent unambiguous assessment of their causal influence, but it does not prevent the researcher from learning something about what can be expected if such events occur under the contemplated policy programs with which they are experimenting.

Third, policy researchers realize that they often deal with social problems that are, unfortunately, quite resistant to treatment of the sort with which they are experimenting. Moreover, they recognize that it takes a large amount of treatment to bring about a small amount of change. Accordingly, researchers accustomed to the difficulties of bringing about the desired outcomes are somewhat uninterested in a long inventory of events occurring in the external world that conceivably could have influenced the experimental results. For example, in income maintenance experimentation, it is difficult to get overly wrought about a small change in aggregate labor demand when the data are showing little, if any, difference between traditional welfare programs and experimental programs that have substantially different levels of support and different rates at which earned income is taxed. If large-scale policy changes designed to bring about certain results have small effects, it is hard to take seriously the hypothesis that external events somehow did have significant consequences. However, this line of reasoning has an obvious shortcoming. Our information that the problem is resistant to change in response to policy programs comes from observations that could have been misleading due to the influence of extraneous factors. Logically, then, there is no basis for ignoring or depreciating the importance of external factors. Still, the point seems worth making at the practical level. Every conceivable competing explanation for observed results cannot be given equal weight; as such, for many external factors, it is simply not tenable that their separate or combined influence was substantial when programs designed specifically to cause change were able to produce little or no change at all.

Despite the above considerations, policy research is argued to be amenable to experimental study. What is important for our purposes is that, in applying experimental methods to social problem intervention, we encounter some problems and issues that are not generally typical of social science experimentation, or that have a different character when they occur in policy research. It is to these points that I now address myself.

MANIPULATION OF PROGRAM INPUTS

A first point concerns the researcher's ability to approach the experimental ideal of independent manipulation of each relevant independent variable in order to ascertain its consequences, or its main effects, and its interactions with the other experimental variables. Here the problem is more complex than is the traditional issue of being unable to manipulate important social variables, because now, such manipulation is seen as impractical and even uninteresting at some level. This follows from the fact that a single policy treatment is typically characterized by a host of variables. For example, in an income maintenance experiment, in addition to the level of guaranteed income and the tax rate on income, there are rules that slide the guarantee for different family sizes, rules governing benefits received by members of a household from other sources (e.g., social security or veterans programs), rules that determine just who can and cannot be counted as members of a household, and other rules as well. There are standard ways of reporting income such that the periodic transfer payments can be made, and should errors or noncompliance occur on the forms, there must be administrative procedures for dealing with the problems. Additionally, the length of the period (called the accounting period) over which income is computed for purposes of calculating the transfer payment needed to maintain the family at their guaranteed income level must be set. Rules must be established to govern the way in which windfall income or large expenditures affect transfer payments over time. These are only some of the additional features which, taken all together, constitute the treatment condition.

Clearly, the researcher is faced with a dilemma. These variables are often highly important either because they affect the dependent variables, because they affect program costs and efficiency, or both. Yet, in any given instance, it may be too expensive to manipulate all of the related programmatic variables. Even if each programmatic variable has only a few discrete levels or conditions of interest, the cost of a full factorial design crossing even a half dozen such variables with the primary experimental and blocking variables becomes prohibitively expensive, particularly in light of the problems discussed in the section of this paper examining problems of sample size. It is true that experimental designs can be employed that do not have all the possible treatment combinations included. For example, fractional replication can substantially decrease experimental costs, but the gain comes at the expense of confounding some higher order interactions with main effects and lower order interactions (see Winer, 1971: 676). If these effects are small relative to main effects and lower order interactions, the loss is tolerable. But often that cannot be known prior to doing the experiment. For some policy experiments it would be possible to design a sequence of fractional replications, letting the results at each stage determine the additional replications needed to reduce the ambiguities imposed by the purposeful confounding. However, the relatively long-term nature of most policy experiments makes this alternative unfeasible.

The other approach to the problem of too many relevant variables is to fix the rules and procedures at a single level thought to be a prime candidate for the proposed program. More will be said about this in the section on administrative experimentation, but it should be clear that the ability to choose these levels or conditions prior to experimentation is not at all beyond question. However, two related risks must be noted. First, the ability to generalize to conditions other than those under which the experiment is conducted is compromised. Second, alternative conditions could very well have substantially different effects and different costs associated with them, but the differences will not show up unless the conditions appear as experimental variables. The obvious methodological shortcoming of not manipulating the program conditions is often not as important in policy experimentation as it would be in basic research. A single example will illustrate this point. In income maintenance experimentation, respondents have transfer payments calculated on the basis of prior information and information about the current month's income. The income is reported on a standard form called an IRF, the Income Report Form. Reporting all of a family's income in this systematic fashion may make people more aware of their ongoing financial situation than otherwise would be the case. As a result, they may change earning behavior or expenditure behavior because of the degree to which they are aware of their financial status. The question arises: should members of the control group fill out the IRF? If they do, then whatever differences are found between controls and experimentals must be due to treatment or random error, but not to the fact that one group reported on their income stream and one did not. This approach assumes that it is important to have an experimental effect uncontaminated by reporting procedure differences. On the other hand, the more important question might be the difference between the effects of the current welfare system, as represented by the control group, and the alternative systems, represented by the experimental groups, all things considered. Since the current welfare programs do not require this form of income accounting, and since any contemplated national income maintenance program would, it can be argued that there is no point in considering experimental effects separate from reporting effects because any national program will have to confound them anyway. This points out an interesting aspect of some forms of policy experimentation: confounding of some factors may be completely acceptable to the researchers. In basic research, surely, the confounding would be considered a flaw, but in some cases of policy research it simply represents an awareness that the program, if instituted nationally, would inevitably confound the factors. To draw the conclusions relevant for policy planning, it is unnecessary to attempt to untangle the effects.[1]

SPECIFICATION OF THE TREATMENT

Throughout the preceding section, the discussion assumed that the sole source of ambiguity in the independent variable set resulted from the confounding of some factors. There is yet another somewhat subtle way that the nature of an experimental variable may be hidden. To an experimentalist, the treatment in policy experiments may seem strange indeed. Precisely, what is the stimulus? In income maintenance experimentation, the entire configuration of guarantees, tax rates, reporting rules, family composition rules, and all the factors discussed in the preceding section together compose the treatment conditions. Similarly, in other types of policy experiments, the treatment may be some combination of various programmatic features of the experimental policy. When this is the case, the experimental character of the research departs somewhat from the classical laboratory experiment, and the nature of the departure is important. First, it is important to ask if the treatment really should be equated with the configuration of rules and procedures. If so, then the stimulus is far removed and abstract in comparison to traditional experiments. After all, one might argue that subjects actually are responding to the treatment they receive rather than to the rules governing the administration of the treatment. So, for the case of income maintenance research, it may be that people are responding to the amount of the checks they receive rather than to the complex of rules and procedures used in calculating the checks. Asked differently, with respect to what factors are experimental subjects homogeneous? The issue becomes relevant because it is quite possible for subjects in different experimental groups to get precisely the same transfer payment because they earned different amounts, because they have different family sizes, because of the carry-over adjustments from prior accounting periods, and because of yet other factors. If it is assumed that the rules and a respondent's past behavior are all part of a cognitive set into which a transfer payment enters, then it is reasonable to consider people receiving identical checks as having undergone different treatments. In fact, it does seem reasonable to think that the rules and the past earning behavior have some influence and that the amount of the check per se is not the treatment. But this raises the issue of what exactly constitutes the stimulus, for if the respondents do not understand the rules of operation, or if they misunderstand those rules, then it becomes difficult to justify treating the actual rules and procedures as if they are the experimental conditions.

In fact, evidence of the problem of respondents failing to understand the rules of operation leads the various income maintenance experiments to attempt to measure level of understanding. Such questions as these were asked of participants: Does a respondent know what payment will be received if the family earns no money? What proportion of each dollar earned does a respondent keep? At what point do all benefits stop? How does the addition or deletion of a family member affect the guarantee level? In one of the experiments, an attempt at a short tutorial was made in order to attempt to bring all respondents up to some minimal level of understanding. For the other experiments, the level of knowledge was measured, but no tutorial was attempted. The measurement was made to provide data that could be used as a control variable in modeling labor supply, consumption, and other outcome variables. The problem of level of understanding became quite important when it was found that a great many respondents simply did not understand the rules governing the calculation of transfer payments. Clearly, if a subject does not understand the rules of operation, then a wise researcher must necessarily ask: what is the nature of the stimulus?

Among some economists, one answer to this question takes a form resembling the behaviorist position in psychology. These economists argue that they do not care what goes on in the head of the experimental subject. The rules are set (the stimulus) and the outcomes (the response) are measured. If the experiment is properly designed, then the conclusions needed to set policy can be drawn. For the policy maker, the argument is made that it is more important to know what the effect of a new policy will be and less important to know why that effect occurred. The relative merits and shortcomings of this approach have been the subject of a lengthy and well-documented debate in the behavioral sciences; thus, the case need not be reviewed here. As a methodological strategy, the behaviorist position obviates the necessity for measuring cognitive states, a difficult measurement task. Moreover, if reliable behavioral laws can be established using only stimulus and response events, with no reference to cognitive events or states, then it may be unnecessary to pursue the more illusive variables. One can easily see that for policy research, such a position can be particularly persuasive, for here even more than in basic research the interest is in the outcomes, not in the mechanism that produced the outcomes. However, there are three difficulties associated with this position.

The first occurs because of the nature of many models being used in the analysis of work-leisure decisions. When justifications for using particular models are made, they implicitly include some presumptions of rational calculus on the part of the subject. For example, the models often assume that the subject understands what the marginal return on an hour of work will be, and further, that the return is weighed against the alternative of taking the time as leisure. If such assumptions are made, then whether or not subjects understand their net wage rates is important and the retreat to a form of economic behaviorism is more difficult to justify. A second problem with the behaviorist approach is that for short duration experiments, external validity may be jeopardized. For policy experiments that provide subjects with benefits of some sort, the rules and procedures may be sufficiently complex that few participants understand how to maximize their benefits under the program. That understanding surely would come in a national program because concerned groups and individuals would make an effort to inform the eligible populations about ways in which to maximize benefits. Over a period of time, the level of understanding would rise as would the total benefits delivered. Thus, estimates based on short-term experimentation could be quite misleading. A third difficulty with the behaviorist approach is that it may fail to measure variables which play an important role in determining the behavior under investigation. The issue goes more deeply than the obvious statistical concern of decreasing error variance by including relevant controls in the regressor set, thereby making it easier to detect experimental effects. While the statistical concern is important, there is the additional fact that some of the unmeasured variables may be manipulatable in real policy programs. The assumptions made by participants about how their behavior influences the benefits they receive and the decision-making rules they use in arriving at courses of action are at least in principle amenable to change. If no attempt is made to measure or model the important cognitive components of economic and social behavior, then one may lose the chance to identify factors and processes that have higher probabilities of leading to socially desirable outcomes.

There is yet another way that some policy experiments encounter difficulty in conceptualizing the explanatory variables, and the problem is related to the previously discussed issue of deciding precisely what distinguishes controls from experimentals. The issue arose in income maintenance research during consideration of alternative models. The two experimental variables were level of guaranteed annual income and the rate at which income is taxed. These variables appeared in practically every model. Even within the domain of the general linear model, there were many ways to specify the model, most of which differed from one another only in the ease with which some interpretations could be made. Many could be transformed into one another. The concern, however, was not with the model form, but rather with the basic conceptual issues that arose in trying to decide how the treatments should be represented. Consider the tax rate, which broadly defined is the rate at which the subsidy is reduced as the respondent earns income. It would appear that inserting a single tax rate parameter in the model, or at most a set of dummy variables for the various tax rates, would be the straightforward way to specify the model. However, in so doing, several intriguing problems arise.

First, experimental subjects who earn more than a particular amount of money go beyond the "break even" point, the point at which the subsidy is reduced to zero. At that point, respondents are no longer subject to the tax rate to which they were assigned. Instead, they now face the same positive state and IRS tax schedules that people generally face. Tax rate is an experimental variable, but it is exogenous only up to a point; thereafter, it becomes an endogenous variable which is a function of, among other things, the respondent's income, exemptions, and deductions. The model must be complicated to deal with these cases. Even then, it happens that the tax rate for experimentals below their break-even point gets moved off the assigned value because they may be receiving benefits that are income conditioned, thereby creating new implicit taxes. Subsidized housing that sets rent according to income is a typical example, and there are others such as food stamps and some agency specific services. Some of these factors can be controlled by design features, but there remains a residual influence that creates discrepancies between assigned and actual tax rates. When attention turns to the control group, the problem becomes even more complicated. The control group in income maintenance experiments is under whatever welfare system they would encounter had no experiment been done. They face all the income-conditioned benefits and services that make the calculation of the effective tax rate difficult. Moreover, they face the state and IRS positive tax rates. Their tax rate is entirely endogenous since no experimental manipulation affects it and since, among other things, it depends on their earning behavior.

Several problems result. First, one must decide how to represent the tax rate of controls. It seems unreasonable to assume it is zero when it is known to be nonzero. If the control group is set as the deleted group for a set of dummy variables representing tax rates, then all other tax rates can be compared to the controls as a reference group. But some of the controls may be facing tax rates identical to those set for experimentals. If so, why should they be treated differently? One response argues that the experiment should be testing for programmatic differences in the tax rate types, the standard state and IRS, and positive tax versus an assigned rate constant up to break-even, and not in differences in actual rate. The problem with this argument is that most of the economic models of labor supply need a net wage rate in the equation and that rate depends in part on the tax regardless of whether it was achieved or assigned. On the other hand, calculating actual tax rates for controls is complicated and expensive. Moreover, once the tax function is created and put into the equation, the essential programmatic differences between the two kinds of taxing rules vanish.

These problems are not insoluble, but they do serve to emphasize two points. The solutions are expensive and involve increasingly complicated models that move researchers away from being able to interpret a single coefficient in a single equation regression model as the experimental effect. Second, and this point holds more generally for policy experiments, the policy equivalent of a placebo is often hard to produce, conceptually or materially. When this difficulty occurs, the control-experimental comparisons are made more ambiguous than is typical in laboratory experiments.

SAMPLE SIZE

Another set of issues that are perplexing in policy experiments concerns special features of an old problem, inadequate sample size. On the surface, policy experiments appear well off with respect to sample size, or at least well off in comparison to much of social science research. And, in comparison to laboratory experiments that involve 10 to 30 subjects per cell, or even fewer, in a design having 10 to 20 cells, policy experiments seem especially strong with respect to data points. For example, the income maintenance experiments involve hundreds of families; the Gary experiment alone has over 1,700 enrolled families. And yet, experience in income maintenance experimentation suggests that even these relatively large samples may be too small for many purposes. Two aspects of the sample size issue are particularly noteworthy. First, policy research shares with much other social research the problem of a poor signal-to-noise ratio. That is, the outcome variables are difficult to predict in most policy research, be they labor supply, utilization of health care facilities, expenditures, investment in human capital, or school performance. When the research is conducted within an experimental context, typically, the experimental variables alone explain only a small proportion of the total variance in the dependent variable. Even adding a large number of control variables may not result in a large proportion of the variance being accounted for. With a large error term, small experimental effects are difficult to detect. This can be particularly perplexing in policy research in which even small changes in the dependent variable can have important policy implications with attending costs of millions of dollars when projected nationally. For example, suppose an income maintenance program were established with a guaranteed annual income of approximately $3,500 for a family of four.[2] In 1968, the Social Security Administration poverty criteria put over 25 million Americans into the poverty category. The cost of an income maintenance program depends heavily on the labor supply and wage rates of the eligible population. It takes very little arithmetic to see that small errors in estimating labor supply and wage rate, when projected to a population this large, can produce extremely large errors in cost estimates since an individual family of four can cost as much as $3,500 per year in direct cash transfers. When costs run this high, accuracy in estimation is important. Sample size is one way to increase the precision of statistical estimates. However, it is well known that precision increases as some function of the square root of sample size. With families in an income maintenance experiment potentially costing thousands of dollars per year in cash transfers, the increased precision will be expensive. The dilemma is clear. Poor estimation and impaired projection of experimental effects can result in extremely costly errors in estimating the effect of contemplated policies. But to obtain the needed precision may require samples so large that the experimental costs are prohibitive.[3] The tradeoff is a difficult one to calculate.

One way of attempting to increase precision more economically involves rational allocation of sample points in the design space. The use of optimum allocation models for sample design is discussed elsewhere in this journal issue, and will therefore be discussed here only briefly. In their favor, policy experiments may spend thousands of dollars on a single sample point. Therefore, it makes sense to allocate the points in a way that takes into account both precision requirements and the different costs associated with different cells. For example, income maintenance experiments spend comparatively little on families in the control group, while the various cells representing different combinations of tax rate and guaranteed annual income represent progressively increasing costs per experimental unit. If the general form of the response function can be anticipated and if some prior estimates of variance can be made, then it is possible and reasonable to attempt to optimize the allocation of sample points.

The form of the response surface must be known because different forms imply different allocations. If one knew in advance that a dependent variable could be expected to be some unknown but approximately linear function of an independent variable, then theoretically one would need to allocate points at only two levels of the independent variable in order to estimate the parameters of the appropriate linear equation. Practically, one would want to have at least some sample points between the two extreme values of the independent variable as insurance against the chance that the functional form is nonlinear. And, if different costs are attached to different levels of the independent variable, then presumably one would have more of the less expensive points and fewer of the more expensive points. If the function is nonlinear and its approximate form can be estimated, then points can be placed along the independent variable so as to provide data where needed to estimate the parameters of the nonlinear function. For some optimum allocation models, policy weights are used to reflect experimental objectives. The Watts-Conlisk model, for example, requires that policy weights be assigned. This is the allocation model used for several of the income maintenance experiments. Regardless of the particular model used, the argument for some means of rationally placing data points in the design space is strong whenever cost differences are large and something is known about the expected outcomes. The sample size problem and the dilemma it poses make it particularly important to place data where they will be most helpful in meeting experimental and policy objectives while maintaining a respect for the large costs of a single observation.

The above notwithstanding, the use of optimum allocation models presents some important problems. Three issues are particularly relevant: first, any of the prior assumptions may be wrong, i.e., the assumptions about functional form, variances, and even the policy weights may in retrospect appear to have been unwisely chosen. Obviously, the more that is known about a particular problem prior to experimentation, the more likely it is that an optimum allocation model can accomplish its goal of maximizing precision with cost constraints. Second, optimum allocation models are optimum with respect to some one dependent variable. But most policy experiments have more than one outcome variable of interest. For example, in income maintenance experiments, labor supply is of prime importance, but policy makers also want to know the effect of the alternative welfare systems on consumption patterns, investment in human capital, job search, mobility, health and health care practices, and a variety of social and social psychological variables related to quality of life. An allocation that is optimum with respect to one dependent variable may be far from optimum for others. Third, allocation models may exacerbate rather than alleviate the small sample problem. This occurs because policy experiments are often quite complex, involving large numbers of variables. Many of the variables must be coded as sets of dummy variables in order to be used in single equation regression models. To illustrate: in the reports from one income maintenance project, an equation was used that required 59 parameters to be estimated. When a parameter space gets that segmented and sample points have been assigned with an optimum allocation model, it is inevitable that some sectors of the response surface will have their heights estimated with only a few cases, and some cells may be completely empty due to attrition or to exhaustion of eligible assignees at the time of allocation. Thus, unless the response surface is relatively smooth, and this becomes increasingly unlikely as the number of dummy variables goes up, there may be a critical loss in precision, and some interactions may be entirely lost.

The small sample problem is further complicated by problems of missing data. Data can be missing for a variety of reasons: people refuse to participate in policy experiments; they enroll, but drop or get dropped; interviews are skipped, lost, or refused; people die, move, or become incapacitated; and so on. When data are lost after an experiment begins, the loss represents lost information that may have already cost a considerable amount of money in benefits and in prior measurement and administrative costs. More importantly, missing data may compromise both internal and external validity. Validity problems arise whenever data are missing nonrandomly with respect to the independent variables, the dependent variables, or both. To show why this occurs, an example from income maintenance research is provided, although the parallel in other policy experiments is obvious.

Data suggest that people who are comparatively better off financially are more likely to leave the experiment. Presumably, those who need the program for financial support are less inclined to quit, and those who receive little in the way of cash transfers have less incentive to remain in the program. The primary dependent variable is labor supply, and it is reasonable to assume that those heavily involved in the labor force are earning more. Consequently, they are receiving lower transfer payments or none at all. Therefore, they are more likely to quit. Assume now that one effect of the program is to increase work incentive. It follows that labor supply differences between controls and experimentals will have as an alternative explanation the fact that high earners, or those who generally work more, in the experimental group dropped out disproportionately more often.[4] This is one example of the way in which differential attrition can produce spurious differences. It is easy to see that differential attrition also could mask differences or distort them. Internal validity clearly is compromised in such instances. External validity gets compromised whenever the sample is changed by attrition in a manner such that generalization to other populations is impaired.

At the present time, differential attrition poses problems which are statistically intractable. Adjustment procedures exist, but all of them assume that data are missing randomly. If that assumption does not hold, the techniques are inappropriate. (See Anderson, 1975, for a lengthy examination of the missing data problem and a review of the literature on statistical adjustment procedures.) No uniformly accepted solution exists. In the Gary Income Maintenance Experiment, models of attrition are being tested in an effort to understand in what ways attriters differ from nonattriters. Moreover, a follow-up interview is conducted and a cash incentive offered in an attempt to get additional information from attriters about their reasons for quitting and their labor supply since they left. Then, it is planned that one of the several regression adjustment techniques will be used to impute missing values. Almost all of the regression adjustment models are based on the assumption that the people who attrite, had they remained in the experiment, would have behaved like the people they resemble on certain variables who did remain in the experiment. It is the regression alternative to precision matching. Once these estimates are made, the imputed values are treated as real data and the analysis is repeated, even though this method violates the basic statistical assumptions of the adjustment models. It is not done instead of analysis on the intact data set, but in addition to that analysis. The purpose is to set some plausible boundaries for the amount of distortion that could have been produced by differential attrition if one assumes that attriters differ from similar nonattriters only with respect to staying in or leaving the experiment.

The method is a poor compromise, but until better techniques are available for dealing with nonrandom attrition, it seems the best alternative to simply analyzing data known or suspected of having undergone nonrandom attrition. In policy experiments, the problem is particularly bothersome because attrition increases with the length of experiments and policy experiments tend to run longer than most laboratory experiments. In addition, the possible distortions due to differential attrition are magnified when coupled with the small cell size problem discussed above. This results because a cell with only 3 to 5 cases can cause large changes in estimated coefficients in large equation models with the loss on a single case. For now, Cochran's often repeated phrase seems the best summary available: the only real way to solve the missing data problem is not to have any. A sound, but not terribly helpful, diagnosis.

RESEARCH OBJECTIVES

The final two issues to be noted arise in the context of deciding on the number of research objectives to be pursued in a single policy experiment. First, policy experiments differ from most laboratory experiments in that there may be many administrative variables of interest. Alternative ways of organizing and administering policy programs always exist. A different configuration may have a greatly different cost, efficiency, and effectiveness. In some experiments it may be possible to manipulate administrative variables, and to measure costs and the like, in order to inform policy makers about the results of alternative administrative and operational structures. However, this raises the general problem of addressing too many questions in a single experiment. No general answer exists for the question, but what is clear is that, by increasing the number of research objectives, one usually increases proportionally the cost, complexity, and attending inefficiency of an experiment. Second, the issue goes beyond the problems presented by imposing an administrative experiment on top of a policy experiment, for even the policy experiment will present researchers with difficult decisions about the number of outcomes to measure. On the one hand, the economy of a limited objective experiment is appealing. On the other, it is hard to know in advance when important direct or indirect effects of the experimental variables will be missed because the relevant variables were not measured. Accordingly, experiments such as the income maintenance efforts focus on labor supply, but at least some versions of the experiments are examining the effects of an income maintenance program on expenditures, health, education, marital stability, fertility, mobility, quality-of-life measures, and others. Interest is on both the direct effects of the program and the indirect effects acting through labor supply. The multiple objective strategy costs more, but it protects against unanticipated deleterious outcomes of policy programs. And it permits social costs or consequences to be attached to the central economic outcomes.

CONCLUSION

This paper has concentrated on a select set of analytical issues that became problematic in the course of evaluating the effects of an income maintenance experiment. Insofar as such problems threaten the validity of other large-scale policy experiments, these remarks should be generalizable. If the income maintenance experiments represent a trend in national policy research, then it is essential that we devote some attention to the specified problems that remain unsolved.

NOTES

1. In fact, both approaches have been used in income maintenance experimentation. In the experiment that does not require controls to fill out the IRF, there is a special subset of controls who do fill them out thus providing a means of estimating reporting effect in the absence of the treatment effects. In this instance, a full factorial design cannot be used because all experimentals must fill out the forms in order to have their treatment administered.

2. The figure is chosen only for illustration. However, it corresponds closely to the Social Security Administration's 1968 poverty line for nonfarm families (U.S. Bureau of the Census, 1969: 11).

3. For many problems addressed and potentially addressable by social experimentation, the costs of the national programs are huge in comparison to research and development costs involved in trial experiments. Perhaps a paper devoted to a few selected analytic issues is not the place to be polemic, but this author notes that the costs of policy experimentation seem large only because of the relatively impoverished past of social research generally and policy research particularly. In comparison to research and development costs in the areas of defense, weaponry, and military technology, social experimentation is notoriously underfunded, especially in light of the real costs to taxpayers of some of the social problems attacked by policy experiments.

4. The actual case is more complicated than this illustration suggests because it fails to take into account the fact that controls generally have a greater incentive to drop out and that financial need as well as income figures into decisions by experimentals, as do several other factors. However, the actual models of attrition being used are too complex to be useful as illustrations.

REFERENCES

ANDERSON, A. B. (1975) "The missing data problem: an analysis of the problem and review of the literature." Gary Income Maintenance Experiment Working Paper (July).

U.S. Bureau of the Census (1969) "Poverty in the United States 1959 to 1968." Current Population Reports, Series P-60, 68, December 31. Washington, D.C.: Government Printing Office.

WINER, B. J. (1971) Statistical Principles in Experimental Design. New York: McGraw-Hill.

COUPLING RANDOMIZED EXPERIMENTS
AND APPROXIMATIONS TO EXPERIMENTS
IN SOCIAL PROGRAM EVALUATION

ROBERT F. BORUCH
Northwestern University

*i*t is often presumed that conducting experiments and using statistical approximations to experiments are independent rather than interdependent activities. The same presumption is implicit in most texts on quantitative methods of assessment. Highly regarded books on experimental design, for example, provide no explicit guidance for developing approximations to experiments, although they often recognize the common models underlying each perspective. Similarly, much of the work focusing on approximations to experiments or on quasi-experiments usually provides no information about how to couple randomized experiments with the approximations. The result seems to lead field evaluators to believe that they must choose between an experiment or an approximation to an experiment in any particular evaluation study. But are the two approaches mutually exclusive in fact and in principle? The answer is important for designing better program evaluations, if not for adjudicating arguments between the two camps.

Intuition suggests that the answer to the question is no. But what facts and principles can be employed to justify this answer? In the following

AUTHOR'S NOTE: *This is an excerpt of an invited paper read at the 1974 Methodology Institute sponsored by Loyola University of Chicago and the Methodology Section of the American Sociological Association. Background research has been supported under Contract NIE-C-74-0115 with the National Institute of Education.*

remarks, the couplings between randomized experiments and approximations to experiments are discussed. I adhere to a brief topical outline:

- Understanding the data and the method of analysis
- Natural experiments and controlled experiments in tandem
- Experiments within quasi-experiments: component-wise experiments, regression-discontinuity
- Quasi-experiments within experiments
- Holdout treatments

Before I proceed further, some preliminary definitions are warranted. *Experiment* refers to the process of randomly assigning experimental comparison of program differences on some response variable and permitting a quantification of confidence in that comparison. An *approximation to an experiment* refers to any statistical technique which does not include the randomization feature, but which is purported to yield fair comparisons and (possibly) quantification of comparisons. However, for heuristic purposes, one can split up the relevant methodologists into three camps: adjusters, fitters, and designers. Adjusters use techniques such as matching, regression, and covariance in order to obtain comparison groups that are alleged to be equivalent to the program recipient group. The fitters group primarily includes methodologists with an interest in structural equation models (e.g., Goldberger, 1973); the models are developed so that "each equation represents a causal link rather than a mere empirical association." The designer group is exemplified by the quasi-experimentalists, who, unlike the typical members of the adjusters or fitters groups, may be able to structure the program evaluation so as to reduce inferences to the lowest level of equivocality possible, without randomization (e.g., Campbell, 1969). The statistical models which underlie analytic methods in each category, of course, are related. The distinctions are offered here only for convenience.

UNDERSTANDING THE DATA AND THE METHOD OF ANALYSIS

The first type of coupling between experiments and approximations to randomized experiments is pedagogical in function and geared chiefly toward understanding the limits of statistical manipulation. Here, one appealing strategy is to locate (or conduct) a randomized experimental test of a program, and in addition, to collect sufficient nonrandomized data to support ostensibly appropriate quasi-experimental assessment of the same program. Suppose, for example, that data are obtained on individuals who have been randomly assigned either to a treatment program (T) or to a control condition (C). Similar data are also collected on an additional group (C') whose members, though not randomly assigned, are regarded as an appropriate comparison group, i.e., "equivalent" in most respects to members of the C group and to the T group prior to treatment. The question is then posed: How does the estimate of program effect based on ordinary analysis of variance of the T-C groups compare with an estimate of effect based on the T-C' groups and conventional statistical techniques such as matching, covariance analysis, or change scores analysis? The answer is important insofar as it helps us to understand the nature and direction of bias that may be obtained when using techniques such as covariance analysis purportedly yield unbiased estimates of effect without randomization.

This idea is not original, and we can acknowledge several planned efforts along these lines. Consider, for example, the Deniston-Rosenstock (1972) reanalyses of data which stemmed originally from a randomized experimental assessment of the Michigan Arthritis Program. The purpose of the Michigan experiment was to permit good judgments about an arthritis program's effects on program participants. To gauge the usefulness of alternative statistical approximations to the experiment, Deniston and Rosenstock conducted pretest-posttest analyses (simple comparison of temporal changes in severity of condition) of the treated group and discrepancy analyses (comparing actual versus predicted severity) for the treated group; they also used a covariance adjustment approach using a C' group chosen post hoc on the basis of similarity to members of the treated group prior to treatment. As one might expect, the magnitude and the sign of the estimated program effect vary depending on the approach one uses, and moreover, estimates based on each statistical approach differ from that yielded by the analysis of fully randomized groups.

Given any approximation to an experimental design, the consequences of violating the assumptions underlying that approximation can and should be worked out beforehand. The main difficulty of doing so in this case, as in most other evaluations, lies in identifying the most plausible violations and gauging their magnitude. For example, the potential misspecification in using the pretest-posttest or covariance approaches in the arthritis data could not be anticipated completely for the T-C' data. And misspecification is especially likely to be the case in an evaluation of a novel program aimed at an idiosyncratic target population. Despite its limitations, this type of study does give the evaluator some feel for the nature of biases which may arise in similar studies and may permit good secondary analyses of quasi-experimental evaluations of some other arthritis research. Not that the approach is perfect. We can always argue that a C' group was chosen incorrectly, that a virtuous path analyst might have included different variables in the analysis, that any right-thinking statistician would not have used the methods that Deniston and Rosenstock used to estimate program effects. These are important points, but they do not vitiate the main one: that the influences which are not recognized in *conventional* applications of statistical techniques can often destroy the validity of an estimate of program effect and can bias it drastically.

To illustrate better how biases are generated by various methods of analyzing observational data, several analogous studies have begun. First is the Project on Secondary Analysis administered by Boruch, Wortman, and Cook (1974). As part of their efforts to reanalyze sets of data, estimates of effects of nutrition, education, and other programs were obtained from randomized (T-C) field experiments. Then, 10 to 15 estimates of effect based on nonequivalent comparison groups, time series, and other available information are computed in order to identify the sensitivity of various estimators to problems of misspecification, error in measurement, and so forth. Focusing on the same problem, Berk (1974) has taken a somewhat different tack: he obtains experimental data, denigrates its quality, and then compares various methods of accommodating the degenerate data with respect to biases in estimators. The results of works such as the two noted are now being used handily in graduate level courses, in some in-service training programs, and in consultation sessions with staff of programs that are being evaluated.

NATURAL EXPERIMENTS AND CONTROLLED EXPERIMENTS IN TANDEM

The second function of coupling experiments to more approximate methods involves the collection of data which bear more directly on making real-world decisions about the effects of a program under evaluation. Several activities are relevant here: finding and using "natural" instances of randomization and planning sequences of controlled randomized experiments and natural experiments.

LOTTERIES AND INSTITUTIONALIZED RANDOMIZATION

Finding and using instances of natural randomization are not easy, but they are not impossible either. For example, any fair lottery is a controlled randomization process occurring in a natural setting. In the simplest case, this presents social scientists with the opportunity to estimate the psychological, economic, and social impact of armed services on individuals in a crude (but unbiased) way if a draft lottery is as advertised. Similarly, one might estimate the effects of special social boons in an unequivocal way for land lotteries (e.g., in the Philippines), hitch-hike lotteries (e.g., in Poland), and others; Sechrest (1970) presents a fine rationale for this type of research. The search for controlled randomization in natural settings is interesting in its own right and does provide an opportunity to assess unequivocally the impact of some social programs.

More importantly, examining such processes can help us to understand more about how randomization can be institutionalized when and where necessary. No systematic research on this topic exists. However, preliminary investigations by Hendricks and Wortman (1974) and others suggest that the acceptability of randomization to an audience can be explored in a limited but informative way through laboratory and small field experiments. Furthermore, institutionalization of randomized experimental tests of social programs may not be as difficult as one might think. For example, one key factor in acceptability of randomization appears to be the individual's physical participation in the randomization process, an easy accommodation in many evaluation settings.

NATURAL RANDOMIZATION AND LEAP-FROG DESIGNS

The discovery of natural randomization more germane for evaluation research involves instances of uncontrolled randomization and more conventional social programs, i.e., cases in which individuals are assigned apparently randomly to one of two or more programs. We recognize that the assignment can never be random if randomness is defined operationally; e.g., randomization is produced by assigning experimental units to treatment on the basis of a table of random numbers. Nonetheless, it is intuitively appealing to regard some processes in society as naturally random, and to capitalize on the intuition to develop procedural approximations to true experiments.

For example, the first stage of Daniels's (1968) evaluation of the DANN mental health program involved assigning incoming patients to an experimental ward or to a control ward on the basis of number of beds available in each. Controlled (deliberate) randomization was introduced at a later stage, following stabilization of ward turnover rate. No significant differences in means or covariances appeared between experimental and control group members within-stage or between the two stages prior to treatment for any of the measures used. As I understand it, estimates of treatment effect based on separate analyses were virtually identical, so data from the two stages were combined to obtain a pooled estimator. This is not to say that the finding of "no significant differences" in means and covariances between the naturally occurring groups prior to treatment should lead directly to pooling or to a flat statement that the groups were naturally randomized. It is to say that there exist situations in which there is no discoverable difference between "naturally" occurring groups and randomly allocated groups, and, moreover, the result of imposing the same simple model on each data set yields virtually the same estimate of treatment effect.

If this coincidence of estimates can be anticipated, then we might plan systematically to capitalize on it. In the simplest case, randomized experiments and nonrandomized setups may be mounted in sequence to verify that each yields estimates of program effect of roughly the same size and sign. For example, Goodwin and Sanders (1972) conducted a series of quasi-experimental and experimental assessments of the effectiveness of tape-recorded lessons for use on school buses. The first test, a quasi--experiment, involved selecting a control bus and a treatment bus whose student riders differed little, if at all, on a variety of measures including a pretest. A covariance analysis resulted in the inference that students were profiting in fact from the tapes. A subsequent randomized experiment involved random allocation of children to treatment bus versus classroom for short periods to verify initial findings and to appraise differences in school bus composition. Those students receiving the taped information out-performed students who did not. A subsequent quasi-experiment involved a more intensive treatment effort on buses, with control and treatment bus riders not assigned randomly. No initial differences in means or covariance structure appeared between groups, and the ANOVA yielded results in the expected direction.

Here, again, there are inferential problems. Although the effect seems to persist from one stage to the next, the size of the estimates varies a bit, probably because of subtle unmeasured differences in the populations sampled at each stage, and specification errors in the analyses based on the nonrandomized data. In any event, the crucial point is that the quasi-experimental estimates of program effect can be matched with experimental estimates at least with respect to direction and approximate size of differences in response to the program. Estimates of effect using one methodology are verified in a very crude sense by a more rigorous one, and the verification process can be planned quite deliberately in such leap-frog designs.

NATURAL RANDOMIZATION AND TANDEM DESIGNS

The joint use of experiments and quasi-experiments in program evaluation need not be confined to sequential applications nor to situations in which natural randomization is known to be likely. We have at least one excellent case study of experiments and quasi-experiments being run in parallel to determine the effects of the program (Salk vaccine), and how inferences based on the experimental data might differ from inferences based on the observational (nonrandomized) data. Meier (1972) used randomized tests of placebo versus vaccine where possible, i.e., in those regions where state health authorities approved the randomization feature. And, he used observational controls when randomization was not approved by state officials: vaccinated second graders constituted the treated group, and first and third graders constituted the observed (nonrandomized) control. The randomized experimental tests permitted some confident judgments about the relative effectiveness of the vaccine, unconfounded by systematic self-selection biases. The evaluations based on nonrandomized samples yielded additional evidence that the effect was notable, but the size of the estimated effect based on the nonrandomized data was smaller than the size of the effect based on the randomized data. Finally, comparison of the effects based on the two sets of data furnished empirical evidence for the contention that sampling biases (volunteerism) can lead to a considerable bias in estimates of program effect in research of this type. This example can be used to help one make subjective judgments about the likelihood of similar biases occurring in other nonrandomized studies of vaccines.

COMBINING ESTIMATES OF PROGRAM EFFECT

When experiments and quasi-experiments are run in tandem, it is sometimes possible to combine estimators to produce a precise yet unbiased estimate of program effect. Even if a series of quasi-experiments yielded biased estimators, if there are a large number of these, they can be used to increase the generalizability of findings based on a few randomized experiments. I know of no complete treatment of the topic, but offer a tentative solution in the following remarks.

Consider a situation in which a large number, N, of evaluations are planned, e.g., site-by-site evaluations of Head Start programs. A random sample of m sites are selected to mount randomized experimental tests and nonrandomized tests. Here, m ≪ N to satisfy political needs for minimal randomization. The remaining N − m sites are instructed to employ the same nonrandomized assessment, say, covariance on pretests. Within the m sites, half the subjects (for example) are randomly assigned to treatment or control conditions. The remaining half are permitted to volunteer themselves in or out of the program, to be recruited, and so forth in much the same way that they would volunteer at other sites. This subgroup then evolves like program participants do in the population at large. For each experimental site j, j = 1, 2, ... m, we obtain an unbiased estimate of program effect based on a randomized experiment, $\hat{\tau}_j$, and a biased estimator based on a quasi-experiment, $\hat{\gamma}_j$. The two estimates will be correlated across sites and a regression model of the form

$$\tau_j = \beta\gamma_j + e_j, \qquad e_j \sim I(0, \sigma^2)$$

can be used to link the two kinds of estimates. For all nonrandomized sites in the population, estimators of the effect can also be computed and averaged to obtain Γ, a biased but precise indicator of effect for the entire population. To obtain a precise unbiased estimate of the effect of treatment in the total population, τ, put

$$\tau. = \sum^m \tau_j/m, \, \gamma. = \sum^m \gamma_j/m, \text{ and } \hat{\hat{\tau}} = \tau. + \hat{\beta}(\Gamma - \gamma.).$$

The variance of this estimator is estimated for large N as (Cochran, 1963):

$$\hat{\sigma}_\tau{}^2 = \frac{1 - m/N}{m(m - 2)} \sum_{j=1}^m \left\{ (\hat{\tau}_j - \tau.)^2 - \beta(\hat{\gamma}_j - \Gamma) \right\}^2.$$

The estimate $\hat{\hat{\tau}}$ is, of course, the familiar regression estimator in survey statistics, where, instead of using y's and x's which are usually response variables, we have used statistics which are functions of response variables.

The strategy laid out here is demanding in that it requires that one conduct m randomized experiments, but this has some demonstrable feasibility if we may judge by contemporary experimental tests of the

Emergency School Assistance Act, and others. The additional requirement for a quasi-experiment at the same site is more severe and might be ameliorated by using proxy estimates of a quasi-experimental effect. Of course, similar regression estimators can be used to increase generalizability of experimental results even if the quasi-experimental estimates are unavailable. In this case, γ_j would represent an arbitrary variable or set of variables which is linearly related to the size of treatment effect.

EXPERIMENTS WITHIN QUASI-EXPERIMENTS

There are a variety of ways in which the clever methodologist can decrease equivocality in part of an evaluation, despite the impossibility of decreasing equivocality in the main study. Many of these approaches involve nesting randomized experiments in a larger framework of quasi-experimental or completely nonquantitative evaluation.

COMPONENT-WISE EXPERIMENTS

Despite what may appear to be a need for evaluation of a total social program (i.e., estimation of overall effects), designing an evaluation as a homogeneous activity is often poorly justified. To be specific, the view that a complex program should be (or can be) evaluated using a single randomized experiment is not necessarily profitable. The experimentalist's zeal is not warranted insofar as there already exists a considerable amount of evidence regarding a program's effects and program sponsors or staff believe that evidence, and to the extent that managerial or physical constraints prevent randomization.

On the other hand, there is often ample justification for the view that components of a complex program (rather than the total program) should be tested using randomized experiments. The component evaluations can often be engineered nicely into a larger quasi-experimental framework for assessment. And when conducted properly, they can help to identify how well microelements of a social program are working, even if political or ethical constraints prevent randomized tests of macroelements or of the complete program. For example, those of you who watch the "Electric Company" (on TV) may have noticed that the words, numbers, and letters are broadcast in fairly well-standardized sizes and duration, and these are readily visible in relation to background. Ed Palmer, director of research for Children's Television Workshop, indicates that these characteristics were determined in part by conducting little experiments on alternative word size, for example, during the program's development (CTW Research Department, 1972). Alternative ways of using Palmer's "distractor" methods to sustain the interests of young viewers are similarly tested. Estimates of a program component's effect from microexperiments such as these can sometimes be combined, so long as we believe effects to be additive, to estimate the total effect of the program. In other types of research, small experiments on program components have similarly helped to make decisions about which of several novel training devices are most effective prior to the formal adoption of one device in larger industrial training programs (Holding, 1969), in methodological studies of threats to the validity of analyses (e.g., Welch and Walberg, 1970), in sociomedical studies of communicating medical information (e.g., Kupst, 1973), and elsewhere (see Boruch, 1974).

Component-wise experimentation may also be helpful when large programs are put into the field without considerable prior evidence on effects, but with strong professional or societal belief that the program is indeed effective. Physicians, for example, are often confident that integrated health care systems are good; that is, if "total" health care is delivered to an individual, his health will improve. As methodologists, we might wish to question this judgment as part of the evaluation. "Expert" opinion, however, may prevent one from doing so with a good quasi-experimental approach, much less with any randomized test. Instead, we might look for those elements of the program about which there is some doubt either in anticipating effectiveness or identifying important population parameters. For example, integrated health care delivery systems in lesser developed countries are being supported by the U.S. Agency for International Development. To the extent that nutrition, health care information, and the like are regarded a priori as good, trying to evaluate their total effect by means of a randomized experiment may be an irrelevant exercise at this point in time. Component-wise evaluation is not. No one knows, for example, how paramedics should be chosen (monks, midwives, village elders) or how they should be trained to yield high treatment rates with minimal cultural disruption. The situation presents us with an opportunity to appraise alternative recruitment and training strategies even if we do not obtain unequivocal data on the actual product delivered by the trainees. It is an obvious compromise of goals (and of the patient's health) if we are unwilling to accept the physician's judgment about the effects of health services. But with at least a foot in the door, better estimates of more fundamental effects may be easier to obtain at some later stage of the research. The physician is more likely to trust the methodologist to do more iconoclastic work if he is judicious in evaluating components which are relatively innocuous.

Component-wise experiments do have some utility beyond the immediate objective of estimating effects for the sample of program recipients at hand. One simple use of the data pertains to disseminating a social program developed initially as a package to be exported to other sites. For example, experience-based career education programs for adolescents are being developed with National Institute of Education funds at four regional educational laboratories. Despite the fact that the programs are complex—they include curriculum materials, special accounting and measurement systems, special communications and organizational schemes—they are supposed to be exportable as well as effective in other geographic areas. The design of replication studies to verify exportability and effectiveness is more manageable if schools that consent to participate in replication studies do not have to adopt the total program, but instead can select the program components that interest them most. To the extent that schools want to adopt components that have not been empirically tested as stand-alones, the original evaluation data (i.e., total program tested experimentally) may be misleading. Individual components may be ineffective or may interact in a substantial way with other components to produce the net effect. The absence of any good data on component effects makes the NIE decision to permit component replication much more difficult than it need be. In the worst case, components which are only marginally effective and perhaps even harmful when used outside the complete package might be adopted.

EXPERIMENTS NESTED WITHIN REGRESSION-DISCONTINUITY DESIGNS

In some situations, an individual's eligibility for a social program is judged on the basis of an explicit continuous scale. For example, a child's eligibility for Head Start is based in part on his parents' income level. A student's eligibility for scholarship may be based on both grades and financial need. A cutting point on the eligibility scale is normally used to decide who receives the program. Those whose eligibility scores fall above the point receive the program or award; those falling below do not. Randomized experiments are usually not an acceptable vehicle for estimating program effects in these cases; the program is presumed to be a benefit, and meritocratic rather than egalitarian criteria must be used in awarding the program. Campbell has suggested the following strategy for estimating program effects under these conditions, using limited randomization, without abridging standards for awarding the program (Campbell, 1969; Riecken et al., 1974).

Individuals whose eligibility scores lie in the vicinity of the cutting point are by definition marginally eligible to receive the program. If measures of eligibility are imperfect and the cutting point itself is known to be a fairly arbitrary matter within those same limits, then assignment of individuals to the program is also an arbitrary matter within those limits. Similarly, if eligibility measures are imperfect and their fallible character is acknowledged in an interval above and below the cutting point, assignment of individuals whose scores fall in this interval is de facto an arbitrary matter. In either case, randomization of individuals with eligibility scores falling within the ambiguous interval can often be justified on grounds of equity. That is, randomization is an explicit recognition of our inability to discriminate well in a narrow band of eligibility. To do otherwise lends a specious and misleading legitimacy to an eligibility score in that interval. When this limited but randomized assignment can be accomplished, one can obtain a clearly interpretable estimate of the program effect for a stratum of the eligible population. At best, the evaluator will have an estimate of effect for the entire range of eligibility, provided that the program effect is completely additive.

The feasibility of the strategy has been demonstrated nicely in British studies (Mather et al., 1971) of the effects of hospital versus home care on heart attack victims. In this experiment, physicians judged victims as being most eligible (critically ill) for hospital treatment, least eligible (sent home), and marginally ill (random allocation to home or hospital). A similar tactic appears to have been used by Sackett (1973) in studies of the effectiveness of nurse-practitioners using regular physician care as a control condition. The model underlying analysis of the randomly assigned, marginally eligible individuals is clear. More sophisticated models can be developed, using the randomized groups as an anchor, to recognize linear relations between eligibility and the individuals' condition at a later time.

A simple extension of these ideas involves nesting experiments within one type of quasi-experimental approach—regression-discontinuity designs. Recall that the basic regression-discontinuity design involves the situation in which individuals are assigned to or deprived of a program on the basis of eligibility. To implement the design, data are collected not only in eligibility, but also on some dependent variable for both recipient and nonrecipient groups. That variable must be an important one for judging impact of the program and must be correlated with eligibility. For example, eligibility for a compensatory reading program might be determined by children's scores on a reading test in September; the criterion variable might be reading tests in June, following the program implementation. In the absence of any program or program effect, the situation is as illustrated in Figure 1a. If the program did have an effect on participants, then a discontinuity in the regression line would emerge; the magnitude of the disruption is a function of the magnitude of program effect (Figure 1b).

One of the main benefits of the design is that, unlike ordinary covariance or matching, one need not assume that reliability of the independent variable (here, eligibility) is perfect or that the mean differences between groups are perfectly specified by observable variables. To obtain an unbiased estimate of the effect, one need only to assume that the reliability of measurement and level of misspecification are comparable for both recipients and nonrecipients, a much less stringent assumption than perfect specification. The less demanding assumption will still be weakly met in many situations, however (see Campbell and Boruch, 1975), and to establish its tenability as well as to guarantee unbiased estimates of effect for certain ranges of eligibility, one can conduct randomized experiments within those ranges. Figure 1c illustrates an experimental test in the marginal range of eligibility. If it is suspected that the curve is nonlinear, then randomized experiments might be conducted at intervals along the eligibility continuum as in Figure 1d. Of course, if all eligible individuals are randomized, then the design boils down to conventional randomized covariance analysis.

So far, attention has been restricted to individual persons as the unit of assignment to programs. Naturally, organizations, cities, and the like can be used in regression-discontinuity designs and perhaps the design is even more feasible for institutions, regions, or groups than for individuals. Again, if groups are used as unit of assignment, randomized assignment of groups within an interval of eligibility may be desirable to assure that competing hypotheses about extraneous variables, differentiability of measures, and so forth do not interfere with estimation or interpretation of the effect. Furthermore, within any given group, randomization of individuals may be possible to estimate effects on individuals within group rather than on groups alone.

QUASI-EXPERIMENTS WITHIN EXPERIMENTS

In some evaluations, randomization of one type of unit is excessively difficult, but randomization of a group of such units is not. The evaluation

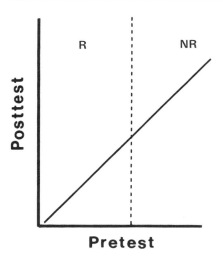

Figure 1a. Null case, sharp cutting point; R = Recipients, NR = Nonrecipients.

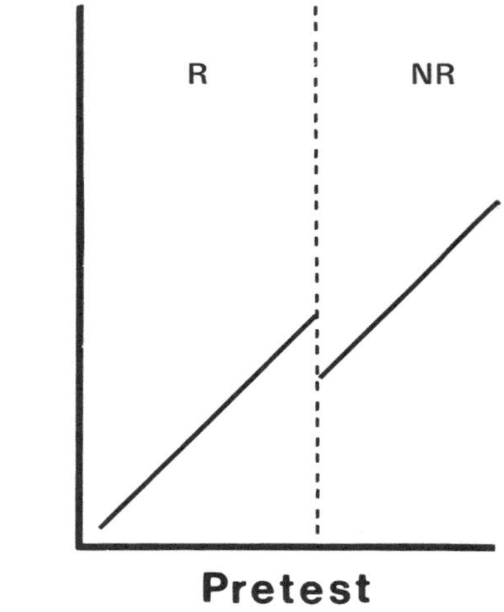

Figure 1b. Nonnull case, sharp cutting point.

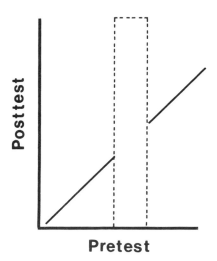

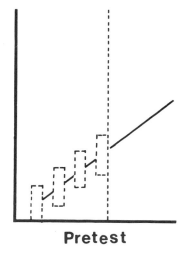

Figure 1c. Null case, randomization in interval at the margin.

Figure 1d. Null case, randomization in selected intervals.

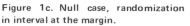

Figure 1.

of the Emergency School Assistance Act seems to be a case in point. Federal money was supplied to school districts for developing compensatory education programs, and interest lay in determining the effect of such support on children's performance on achievement tests. Randomly assigning children to a program within a school was judged not feasible in this particular case. As a compromise design, eligible districts were identified on the basis of needs of children they served, and then eligible schools were assigned randomly to receive funds until all funds were expended. The net result is an experiment using an organizational unit of analysis and using mean test scores of subsets of children within school as a major response variable. The experiment is an indirect one vis-a-vis the main target population, disadvantaged children. But it is direct insofar as it yields clear estimates of the effect of the increased financial support on groups of children rather than on individual children, estimates which are not confounded systematically with differences in school composition, region, and so forth. The study of the impact of the particular program on children within a school must be based on observational (nonrandomized) data. But at least some sturdy randomized data are available to justify even looking within schools for promising approaches to compensatory education.

The last remark suggests, among other things, that examining within-school regressions of cognitive test scores on intensity of treatment can be useful. By intensity here we mean a measurable indicator of how much special education a child received, e.g., hours spent in special tutoring, self-reports of depth of program, reports by teachers on their perception of how well the program was received by children, and so forth.

Using indicators such as these in simple correlational or other quasi-experimental assessments within group can help to achieve several ends. Perhaps the most important is improving the power of analysis of data based on the randomized samples. To illustrate, suppose that in nature the treatment is imposed with some variation about a fixed mean. Furthermore, suppose that these subtle variations within group produce some real variation in response. A specific characterization might take the form:

$$Y_{ij} = \alpha + \beta_B X_{.j} + \beta_W (X_{ij} - X_{.j}) + e_{ij}$$

$$i = 1, 2 \ldots N; \quad j = 1, 2; \quad e \sim I(0, \sigma^2).$$

Here, i indexes child within treatment group, j indexes treatment group or control, $X_{.j}$ is a dummy variable for treatment (+1) and control (−1) with correspondent regression coefficient, β_B. The variations in intensity of treatment within group are signified by $(X_{ij} - X_{.j})$ and these are linked to responses Y_{ij} through the coefficient within groups, β_W. Because $X_{.j}$ and $X_{ij} - X_{.j}$ are independent, estimates of β_B and β_W are simple:

$$\hat{\beta}_B = \frac{\Sigma(X_{.j} - X_{..})(Y_{.j} - Y_{..})}{\Sigma(X_{.j} - X_{..})^2} = \frac{\Delta Y}{2}$$

$$\hat{\beta}_W = \frac{\Sigma(Y_{ij} - Y_{.j})(X_{ij} - X_{.j})}{\Sigma(X_{ij} - X_{.j})^2}.$$

Each estimator is unbiased if X_{ij} is regarded as a fixed variate; β_B is unbiased if $X_{.j}$ is fixed; and β_W is unbiased if $X_{.j}$ is fixed and X_{ij} is random and measured reliably. The population variance of $\hat{\beta}_B$ is

$$\text{Var}(\hat{\beta}_B) = \frac{SS_e}{2N\Sigma(X_{.j} - X_{..})^2}$$

where $SS_e = \Sigma(Y_{ij} - \alpha - \beta_B X_{.j})^2 - \beta_W^2(X_{ij} - X_{.j})^2$.

Now if the variations $X_{ij} - X_{.j}$ were ignored as they usually are in ordinary analysis of randomized experiments, the ordinary model

$$Y_{ij} = \alpha' + \beta' X_{.j} + \eta_{ij} \qquad \eta_{ij} \sim (0, \sigma_\eta^2)$$

would lead to an unbiased estimate of effect

$$E(\hat{\beta}') = E\left[\frac{\Sigma(X_{.j} - X_{..})(Y_{.j} - Y_{..})}{\Sigma(X_{.j} - X_{..})^2}\right] = \beta_B$$

But the variance of this estimator will often be larger than necessary.

$$\text{Var}(\hat{\beta}') = \frac{SS_e + \beta_W^2 \Sigma(X_{ij} - X_{.j})^2}{2N\Sigma(X_{.j} - X_{..})^2}$$

$$= \text{Var}\,\hat{\beta}_B + \frac{\beta_W^2\, SS_W}{2NSS_B}.$$

To the extent that the within-group regression, β_W, and the within-group sum of squares, SS_W, are large, then their measurement and removal will increase power of experiments to detect subtle program effects. This notion, of course, is a simple algebraic translation of an old intuition: that clinical judgments, classroom ratings, and the like of processes within a treatment condition can be used to specify better the magnitude of a treatment impact. But it does not rely solely on the within-group regressions implied by clinical intuition; it supplements this with less equivocal between-group regression estimates. To verify both the intuition and its algebraic translation, the Project on Secondary Analysis (Boruch, Wortman and DeGracie, 1974) is conducting reanalysis of data from randomized tests of some social programs. In the evaluation of Middlestart, a precollege program for minority group youth, indicators of treatment were available though they were unused in the original evaluation. A conventional t-ratio for the hypothesis that Middlestart had no effect on level of education yielded a test statistic of 2.56. Using an indicator of reception of treatment—student reports of how well they liked the program—the t-like ratio described above is 2.6, suggesting only a slight increase in power of the analysis.

Insofar as there is no relation between test scores and randomly occurring levels of intensity within group, we may choose to regard this as a Berkson case. If within-group regressions appear to be parallel to the between-group regression, then combining estimates may be reasonable; we might tentatively regard even small increments in level of treatment as completely additive, and we might pool the between- and within-group estimators to obtain a more stable estimator of the overall program effect.

We are, however, more likely to find that the between- and within-group regressions are not parallel. There are a great many potential explanations for a difference between β_B and β_W; some of them may bear further scrutiny. For example, the total relation between test scores and intensity may be a step function suggesting that treatment increments below a particular amount will have no noticeable effect on children. Or the functional relation may be curvilinear. Changes in treatment intensity at the extremes of treatment may have little impact by comparison to changes at the intermediate level of intensity. The within-group regression parameters may be smaller than the between-group regression parameter simply because there is more error of measurement within group—fine distinctions among intensity levels are less reliable than coarse (all or none) distinctions—or because very high or very low intensities cannot be measured with available indicators.

Finally, within-group regressions may be useful in judging the credibility of estimates of the effects of other special programs. One may find that estimates of within-group regression for the experiment at hand match fairly well with estimates of the effect of evaluations of the same program at other sites based on nonrandomized data. To the extent that this is true and within-group regressions differ from the between-, then one has some additional grounds for contending that the estimators based on nonrandomized data from evaluations of similar social programs are biased.

HOLDOUT TREATMENTS

One of the unfortunate interpretations of classical experimental design is that the administration of treatment is an all or none affair; i.e., an individual either receives treatment or he does not. Confronted with social or political pressures to admit all candidates to a new social program, the evaluator may simply assume that a randomized assessment is impossible and then design a quasi-experiment to estimate program effects. Several important opportunities for randomization often present themselves, however, when a simplistic notion of "experiment" is abandoned. Two important classes of alternatives involve the use of holdout treatments.

In the simplest holdout approach, a subset of individuals is randomly selected from the program's pool of eligible candidates to serve as a control group. The majority of candidates participate in the program immediately, while program participation is delayed for the control group members. The use of a temporary holdout sample can often be justified on managerial grounds: new social programs often do not have substantial budgets and cannot always accommodate (at a given point in time) all applicants to the program. To the extent that each eligible candidate has an equal right to the program, randomized delays can be justified on equity grounds.

In some cases, the accessible target population is so small that a holdout sample would be predictably too small to be useful. Depending on the program it may be possible to increase accessibility to the target population and subsequently to increase size of the holdout sample. Crude devices for doing so include increasing the effort to recruit candidates for the program and paying control and program group members. Both tactics have been used with some success by the NIE-supported career education programs at the Northwest Regional Laboratory. Altering recruitment strategies changes the character of the program a bit, but insofar as both experimental and control groups are treated similarly in this respect, the estimates of program effect are still unbiased. To the extent that increasing accessibility redefines or expands the original target population, then the experiment yields an unbiased estimator with respect to the new population and a biased estimator with respect to the original one. The original target population for any social program is usually not the same as the one the program actually winds up serving, however, and the increased emphasis on (and support for) recruitment of candidates for the program is consistent with most program developer goals.

A straightforward generalization of the holdout treatment notion is to tailor the experiment so that as the program's ability to accommodate candidates increases, more members of the randomized control group members are periodically assigned to the program. The gradual depletion of an initially fixed size control group might occur as a batch process, i.e., small subgroups randomly taken from the control and placed in the program as time goes on. Or, we might employ trickle processing, i.e., unit-wise deletion of control group members. The process is schematically illustrated in Figure 2a. Which tactic one chooses depends on conditions in the field; e.g., a sociomedical program for the chronically ill may make slots available as beds become available, a trickle process (see Riecken et al., 1974).

Note that the presumption made here is that every eligible volunteer candidate must ultimately enter the program, regardless of the actual program effects. The requirement is often explicit in political, ethical, or legal mandate for the program. What is usually implicit, however, is that delay of treatment is possible, perhaps even necessary, for managerial reasons. The experimenter can take advantage of these delays, for scientific reasons, provided that he knows enough about project management to identify the sources and character of delay.

The genuinely randomized stage-wise experimentation strategy described here can be tied readily to other methods of estimating program effects. Figure 2b illustrates how either batch processing or trickle processing can be represented as a short time-series design. In the upper set of curves, each curve represents the mean response level of a group when membership is determined by random assignment from the pool of eligible candidates. The assignment is gradual with increases in elevation, suggesting increases in mean response to immediate imposition of treatment. The lower set of curves is more complicated and more realistic representation with group means reaching asymptotes and then temporarily eroding to a second asymptote, and is presented to illustrate the intractability of

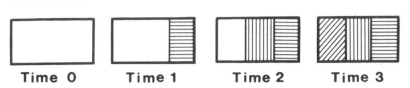

Time 0   Time 1   Time 2   Time 3

Figure 2a. Incremental randomized assignment from control group to treatment (shaded) group.

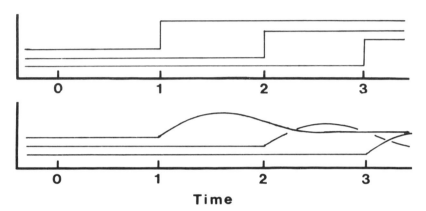

Time

Figure 2b. Time series framework.

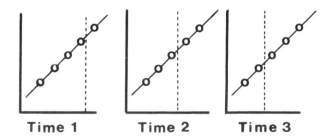

Time 1   Time 2   Time 3

Figure 2c. Regression-discontinuity framework.

Figure 2.

estimation problems when one relies on short time-series design alone. Figure 2c illustrates a further generalization of the holdout sample notion, this time in the context of regression-discontinuity design. In year zero, prior to formal field tests of the program, cities are arranged according to need for a program. In year one, only the most eligible are supported in their efforts to implement the program; year two, the two most eligible categories of cities have been funded; and so forth. The design helps to obtain estimates of short-term impact, intermediate impact, and longer-term impact of the program on cities, and if necessary randomized tests can be run within category or at the margin to decrease equivocality of inferences based on the design.

A second major variation on the holdout treatment approach involves the situation in which the use of a no treatment control condition, temporary or otherwise, is completely unacceptable. In this case, it is often possible and desirable to encourage tests of alternative levels of treatment and extrapolation to no treatment control. For example, in an experiment supported by the U.S. Department of Labor, it has been demonstrated that income subsidies given to prison parolees for 13 weeks following prison release can reduce recidivism significantly (Lenihan, 1975). State governments undertaking a replication of the experiment may be unable to employ randomized control and treatment (as in the original study) in evaluating their own efforts. They are, however, likely to be able to employ randomized assignment to alternative levels of treatment, e.g., income subsidies of $65-$85-$135 per week over 13-16-18 weeks. The multilevel approach, in any case, permits better resolution of real policy options if such a program is adopted on a national scale. And if comparisons with control conditions are desirable, extrapolation to a predicted control condition in the sample at hand is possible (but hazardous in this case) if recidivism is a simple (e.g., linear) function of duration and amount of subsidy. In this case, the extrapolated control is realistic in that parolees now receive "$25 and a baloney sandwich," and it will be informative if the functional relation is strong. The hazards here are in other respects similar to those in any functional prediction, e.g., severe discontinuity in the functional relation at the zero subsidy point. Again, this strategy is not a formal randomized test of treatment relative to control. It does involve a change of question to "what is the functional character of impact of treatment?" for the randomized test and to "what is the treatment's impact relative to predicted control?" for the extrapolative test. The latter question is generic to typical nonrandomized tests, but because these, unlike the current proposal, do not attempt to establish the dependence of response on level of treatment through randomized experiments, the question will typically be answered with a biased estimate of effect.

REFERENCES

BERK, R. (1974) "Evaluating evaluations." Presented at Evaluation Colloquium Series, Evaluation Research Program, Psychology Department, Northwestern University, August 13.

BORUCH, R. F. (1974) "Bibliography: illustrative randomized experiments for planning and evaluating social programs." Evaluation 2: 83-87.

–––, P. M. WORTMAN, and T. D. COOK (1974) "Project on secondary analysis: three year plan for research, development, and testing." PSA Research Report. Northwestern University.

BORUCH, R. F., P. M. WORTMAN, and T. S. DeGRACIE (1974) "Executive summary: project on secondary analysis." Presented at annual meeting of the American Educational Research Association, April 2, Washington, D.C.

CAMPBELL, D. T. (1969) "Reforms as experiments." Amer. Psychologist 24, 4 (April): 409-429.

––– and R. F. BORUCH (1975) "Making the case for randomized assignment to treatments by considering the alternatives: six ways in which quasi-experimental evaluations in compensatory education tend to underestimate effects." Extension of a paper presented at Conference on Central Issues in Social Program (C. A. Bennett and A. Lumsdaine, coordinators). Seattle: Battelle Human Affairs Research Center.

COCHRAN, W. G. (1963) Sampling Techniques. New York: Wiley.

CTW Research Department (1972) "Preliminary data from progress testing: memo to producers and advisors." New York: Children's Television Workshop Research Department (January 27).

DANIELS, D. N. et al. (1968) "Dann services program." Research Report. National Institute of Mental Health, Grant 02332 (January).

DENISTON, O. L. and I. M. ROSENSTOCK (1972) "The validity of designs for evaluating health services." Research Report. University of Michigan (Ann Arbor) School of Public Health (March).

GOLDBERGER, A. S. (1973) "Structural equation models: an overview," in A. S. Goldberger and O. D. Duncan (eds.) Structural Equation Models in the Social Sciences. New York: Seminar Press.

GOODWIN, W. L. and J. R. SANDERS (1972) "The use of experimental and quasi-experimental designs in educational evaluation." Research Report. University of Colorado Laboratory of Educational Research.

HENDRICKS, M. and C. WORTMAN (1974) "Reactions to random assignment in an ameliorative social program as a function of awareness of what others are receiving and outcome." Northwestern University Psychology Department.

HOLDING, D. H. [ed.] (1969) Experimental Psychology in Industry. Baltimore: Penguin.

KUPST, M. J. (1973) "Experiments in communication of medical information." Research Report. NIMH HS 00889. Children's Memorial Hospital, Chicago, Illinois. (mimeo)

LENIHAN, K. J. (1975) "The LIFE Project: preliminary results, design questions, and policy issues." Prepared for the Manpower Administration, Department of Labor. Washington, D.C.: Bureau of Social Science Research.

MATHER, H. G., N. G. PEARSON, K. L. READ, D. B. SHAW, G. R. STEED, M. G. THORNE, S. JONES, C. J. GUERRIER, C. D. ERAUT, P. M. McHUGH, N. R. CHOWDHURY, and M. H. JAFFARARY (1971) "Acute myocardial infarction: home and hospital treatment." British Medical J. 3 (August): 334-338.

MEIER, P. (1972) "The biggest public health experiment ever: the 1954 field trial of the Salk poliomyelitis vaccine," in J. M. Tanur, F. Mosteller, W. B. Kruskal, R. F. Link, R. S. Pieters, G. Rising (eds.) Statistics: A Guide to the Unknown. San Francisco: Holden-Day.

RIECKEN, H. W., R. F. BORUCH, D. T. CAMPBELL, N. CAPLAN, T. K. GLENNAN, J. W. PRATT, A. REES, and W. WILLIAMS (1974) Social Experiments: A Method for Planning and Evaluating Social Programs. New York: Seminar Press.

SACKETT, D. L. (1973) "End results analyses in a randomized trial of nurse practitioners." Research Memorandum, Burlington Study Group, McMaster University Medical Center, Hamilton (Ontario).

SECHREST, L. (1970) "Dissipating and snowballing effects in social amelioration: lotteries as true experiments." Florida State University (Tallahassee) Psychology Department. (mimeo)

THISTLETHWAITE, D. L. and D. T. CAMPBELL (1960) "Regression-discontinuity analysis." J. of Educ. Psychology 51: 309-317.

WELCH, W. W. and H. J. WALBERG (1970) "Pretest effects in curriculum evaluation." Amer. Educ. Research J. 6: 605-614.

A number of important methodological issues have emerged from recent large-scale social experiments which have an important bearing on the ultimate usefulness of such research for policy determination. This paper discusses a number of these design issues in the context of the New Jersey Income Maintenance Experiment, focusing on the importance of the shift from conventional to optimal designs for experiments with inherently costly treatments. Risks of optimal designs lie in the possible misspecification of the response surface and the exclusion of important secondary objectives which may be politically important to policy use. The conclusion is that experimentation is a costly research method which compels optimal designs in order to identify generally small treatment effects at the usual significance levels.

SOME OBSERVATIONS ON DESIGN
ISSUES IN LARGE-SCALE
SOCIAL EXPERIMENTS

KATHARINE C. LYALL
Johns Hopkins University

*t*he first of a number of large-scale social policy experiments spawned by the Great Society programs of the late sixties has recently been completed as well as a summary of its results, issued by HEW. The final report of what is popularly known as the New Jersey Income Maintenance Experiment consists of thirty analytical papers and three technical appendixes which attempt to carve out of a mountain of data the rough features of a labor supply response to the tax and guarantee parameters defining a series of eight negative income tax plans. The labor supply effects found were small, inconsistent across ethnic subgroups, and largely unconvincing to congressional policy makers debating the Family Assistance Plan and other national welfare reforms. Tests of secondary hypotheses concerning social, psychological, and demographic effects of a NIT failed to turn up any significant effects on family structure, mental or physical health, or community participation. To some proponents of

AUTHOR'S NOTE: *This article was prepared for the American Sociological Association meetings, Montreal, August 25-28, 1974. The research on which this paper is based is part of a larger evaluation study of the New Jersey experiment funded by the Russell Sage Foundation.*

experimentation as a mode of policy research these results have been disheartening.

To some extent, the inability to draw convincing policy conclusions, positive or negative, from the experimental data can be traced to a series of design decisions which had the effect of subdividing the sample in such a way that responses as small as those found in the final data cannot be interpreted as significant within the usual confidence limits. This paper focuses on one aspect of the experimental design: the process by which a given sample is allocated across a specified number of treatments. The contributions made to the methodology of experimental design by the New Jersey experiment lie here and need to be well understood in light of these results if they are to be properly integrated into the body of knowledge about experimental design in the Fisherian tradition. The following discussion is in no way a comprehensive critique of the NJE; that complex task is being attempted elsewhere.[1] Rather, the NJE is a useful vehicle for talking about experimental design because it is a recent, widely discussed large-scale policy experiment and because the designers of the NJE have made a methodological contribution to experimentation which stands in interesting contrast to more conventional designs and promises to be increasingly important as experimentation is adopted in other realms.

A major methodological contribution of the NJE is embodied in the Watts-Conlisk model for the allocation of a sample among specified treatments. This model shifts the conventional focus of experimental design from the generation of random samples to the construction of optimal designs defined in terms of maximizing the information gained per dollar of experimental budget. Economizing on the experimental budget is a particularly tempting way to design experiments whose treatments are inherently costly, i.e., where treatments are cash transfers. Indeed, variants of the basic Watts-Conlisk allocation have been adopted by the subsequent NIT experiments still under way in Seattle, Denver, and Gary.[2]

The main arguments of this paper trace the impact of this efficiency focus on interpretation of experimental results. The major conclusion is that the modest magnitude of behavioral responses that can be anticipated in social policy experiments dictate a very careful balancing of efficiency and broader criteria in experimental design.

In analyzing the impact of experimental design decisions on the interpretation of results, one thinks of the experimental design process as a series of design decisions, both exclusionary and enabling, ranging from the formulation of the major experimental hypothesis to the structuring of simple administrative and field procedures. In the New Jersey experiment these included decisions to: [3]

(1) structure the experiment as a *single* treatment test (i.e., a test of NIT plans alone), thereby ruling out the possibility of discovering interactions between NIT and other treatments such as manpower training and day care—such composite programs were incorporated in later income maintenance experiments in Seattle, Denver, and Gary;

(2) define the *target population* as work-eligible male-headed families, thereby eliminating tests of the responses of a large percentage of the poor situated in female-headed families and unemployables;

(3) reject a *national probability sample* in favor of a few sample sites (Trenton, Newark, Scranton, and Paterson-Passaic), thereby reducing the ability to generalize to a national population;

(4) specify *urban sites,* thereby introducing the possibility of site bias from special features of those particular labor markets and eliminating generalizations of results to the rural poor;

(5) select a *"randomized"* rather than a saturation sample in each site, thereby eliminating the ability to detect macrolevel labor supply and consumption effects;

(6) define a particular *policy space* in g and r as "feasible," thereby eliminating the detection of direct response outside this range and to other parameters;

(7) select a *particular regression model* (in contrast to a simpler design with equal observations per treatment), embodying certain assumptions about the probable shape of the response surface and the values of its parameters, as the *method by which the sample was allocated* across the eight experimental plans and the control group, thereby introducing the possibility of misspecification error as the price of minimizing inefficiency in use of the experimental budget. The following discussion is concerned with the contributions of the NJE to this last design feature—the efficient allocation of a fixed sample over alternative treatments. Internal debate on this among the researchers themselves became known as the "design controversy."

THE ANALYTICS OF EXPERIMENTAL ALLOCATION

Perhaps the simplest way to comprehend the substance and significance of the design controversy in the New Jersey experiment is to envisage the relevant policy space to be investigated. A policy space is defined by the range of one or more policy parameters deemed of interest to decision makers. In the case of the NIT experiment the relevant policy space was defined over the ranges of g, the minimum income guarantee level, and r, the marginal tax rate on income received above level g, represented in the three-dimensional space of Figure 1. The g equals the minimum income guarantee expressed as a percentage of the officially defined poverty level for a family of four, and r equals the constant marginal negative tax rate to be applied to earnings above g. The Y equals the response measured in earned income, or alternatively, in hours worked.

While any point in this space is possible, only a subset of points represent feasible policy alternatives. In the case of the NIT the feasible range of alternatives was thought to lie between r = 30-70% and g = 50-125% of poverty level, the space outlined in the g-r plane in the diagram. Theoretically, with unlimited budget and resources, virtually the entire policy space could be estimated. In practice, however, this is both unlikely and unnecessary—ordinarily, a discrete number of points or experimental treatments are selected for estimation. The general objective is to estimate the height of the response surface, Y, at each design point in the feasible policy space as well as the slope of the response surface between points.[4] As will be seen below, this estimation process is more efficient under some sets of assumptions about the shape of Y(f) than under others.

Virtually every experiment operates under a budget constraint which in effect determines the size of the total sample that can be used as well as

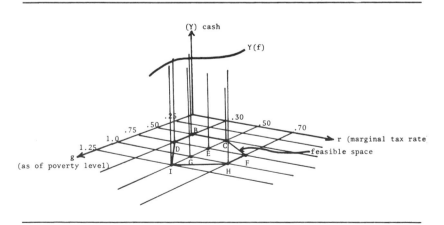

Figure 1: Income Stratum I.

the magnitude of the minimum response that will be detectable at a given significance level. If observations are very expensive, only a small sample can be used, and, accordingly, only relatively large experimental-control differences will be detectable at, say, the 90% to 95% confidence level. This problem becomes especially important where one is not merely surveying the sample (an operation with roughly equal costs per respondent), but actually intervening with a "treatment" which is itself costly—actual transfer payments in the case of NITs, health insurance plans, housing vouchers, and the like—and varying among respondents. In this latter case, the pattern of assignment of observations to plans (treatments) will itself substantially affect the size of the total sample that can be afforded—the experimenter is faced with a tradeoff between fewer observations at relatively expensive points (plans) on the policy space or more observations at cheaper points; the first arrangement implies that a relatively large response will have to be elicited to be detected at a given confidence level, while the second detects a smaller response with the same precision. While the differences in the cost of interviewing respondents in traditional survey sampling studies are not ordinarily very great, in transfer experiments these costs can vary from almost nothing for controls to several thousand dollars per observation per year for those assigned to "generous" plans; extended over a three- to five-year experimental period, these differences can virtually dictate the sample design.[5] In effect, then, the size of the total sample, its allocation across experimental treatments, and the precision with which responses can be detected are interdependent design decisions.

CONVENTIONAL VERSUS OPTIMAL DESIGNS

If a simple analysis-of-variance approach is used, the experimenter will allocate an equal number of observations to each point (plan) in the policy space and, where he is operating under both a sample size and a budget constraint, will assign observations to each point in the ratio of: $1/\sqrt{k}$ ($\sqrt{c_1/c_2}$) controls for every treatment observation, where k is the number of design points and c_1 and c_2 are the costs of control and treatment observations, respectively.[6]

It can be argued that the ANOVA approach to the allocation of the sample is inefficient because, in the case of experiments, we are interested in estimating not just the response to a series of discrete plans, but a continuous response *surface* over the full range of the policy parameters defining the policy space.[7] We are not interested in the particular plans of Figure 1 per se, but in the response to increasing tax and guarantee levels across the whole policy space, and we can be rather sure on the basis of previous experience that there is some continuity in the behavioral adjustments individuals make to income and other changes. If we are willing to assume continuity in the response surface (although its shape is still a matter for empirical estimation), a much more efficient use of the sample N is possible which accommodates the differences in the costs of observations assigned to different plans by concentrating observations at those test points which can provide the most information about the shape of the response surface *per dollar of budgetary cost*.

The import of this shift in an efficiency criterion can best be seen by imagining the response surface Y(f) of Figure 1 to have different shapes. If Y(f) is taken to be planar (i.e., linear) in the g, r, Y space, then only three experimental points need be estimated since three points are sufficient to position a linear surface. As it happens in the NIT case, it is extremely efficient to have one of these three be the control group at the origin (g = 0, r = 0) since control observations are relatively cheap, requiring the payment of only a small reporting fee. Further, it is optimal to select these points at extremes on the edge of the relevant policy space since this will minimize the variance of estimates made from the surface. Middle-income, middle-treatment points are by this criterion inefficient test points.

If, however, Y(f) is assumed to have some nonlinear form, then interior points must also be observed to get an estimate of the degree of curvature in the surface. The higher the degree of the assumed polynomial function describing the response surface, the greater the number of inflection points and the more interior design points must be covered to pick these out.

It is evident from this that the optimal design of an efficient sample allocation is a complex function of the relative costs of observations at different points, the overall budget constraint, and the assumed shape of the response surface. A formal sample design allocation model worked out by Watts and Conlisk (1969: 150-156) for the NJE has largely been accepted as the basic approach for several subsequent experimental allocations, and it is worth noticing its general features and their influence on the interpretation of final results. (The Watts-Conlisk approach has been adopted by the other income maintenance experiments and the RAND health insurance experiment proposal among others.)

THE WATTS-CONLISK MODEL

The Watts-Conlisk model applied to the NJE consists of four functions embodying rather specific assumptions about the behavioral responses of experimental families:

(1) Response Function Z: a basic quadratic response function specifying that the ratio of posttreatment to preexperimental earnings (or hours worked) is a complex function of responses to g, r, g^2, r^2, and the interaction of gr. This particular quadratic formulation permits the detection of a response surface which is concave or convex to the g-r plane (i.e., shows increasing or decreasing response to the experimental parameters), but not one with more complicated contours (i.e., with both increasing and decreasing sections). Simpler (i.e., linear) surfaces can be estimated from data generated from this sample allocation, but not more complex ones so that the selection of a second-degree quadratic for the response function represents a judgment on the part of the experimenters that the response likely to emerge would not be more than a simple monotonically increasing or decreasing rate of change.[8]

(2) Objective Function C: an average cost function for families in each treatment cell, in which cost is defined as all of the transfer cost (the actual NIT payments) attributable to reduced work effort including specific expressions of: differential attrition costs for experimentals and controls [(3) Attrition Function] and a function expressing the probability that a family currently above the break-even level for receipt of NIT payments will drop below and begin to collect payments [(4) Transformation Function]. C_i, then, provides the estimated cost of an observation assigned to each treatment point, and

$$\sum_{i=1}^{k} C_i n_i$$

is the total cost of any given experimental allocation.

Substituting the response function Z into the total cost function produces a nonlinear objective function in terms of g and r the variance of which can be minimized subject to a specified budget constraint (expressed in either dollars or in total number of observations). That is, the model selects that allocation which allows detection of the smallest possible significant variance in earnings (or hours worked) at some confidence level within a given experimental budget constraint.[9]

In order to see the implications of this efficiency focus in the design for interpretation of experimental results, one should examine the allocations generated by the model for the NJE displayed in Table 1. The first two columns show the simple ANOVA and the unconstrained Watts-Conlisk (pure efficiency) allocations. The Watts-Conlisk model produces very unbalanced distributions of the sample concentrating as much as 88% of all observations in a very few "cheap" cells at the extreme edges of the policy space—specifically in the control group (which receives no transfer payments) and at treatment cells in which large numbers of families are above the break-even level (and so ineligible for payments). In such allocations, only about 10% of NIT payment recipients would be drawn from poverty level income strata. This pattern results in part from the focus of the model on assigning observations to plans where they produce the most information for the' least cost (hence, to cheap plans) and in part from the assumption made about the probable shape of the response surface, so that cheap plans at the extremes of the policy space are highly favored.

The relative inefficiency of the equal allocation is dramatically revealed by the indicators shown between the horizontal rules: total sample size that can be afforded with the same budget is less than one-third that of the unconstrained design while the total and average costs are several orders of magnitude higher. At the same time, the unconstrained distribution achieves a very low cost per observation largely by concentrating 70% of all families in the control group with another 18% in the peripheral (and low payment) plans F, H, and I.

RISKS OF AN OPTIMAL DESIGN

The objections to such unbalanced but efficient experimental allocations lie in two areas: (1) the risk of misspecification of the response function Z, and (2) the sacrifice of important secondary objectives of the experiment. Misspecification of the response surface carries the risk that the sample will be concentrated at too few points to detect experimental responses which are significant but more complex than originally anticipated. This is in essence a Type II risk—that experimental results will show no significant response when, in fact, a real but complex response exists. If, for example, we assume a planar surface and consequently test

TABLE 1
Consolidated* Sample Allocations Calculated for Different
Sets of Parametric Assumptions and Constraints by Watts-Conlisk Model
(all allocations within budget constraint: B ≤ $1,450,000)

Tax Plan		Equal ANOVA		No Constraints		$n_i \geq 20$		Multiple** Constraints		Tobin Allocation
g	r		φB		φB		φB		φB	
A	0	0	97	(.01)	2031	(.10)	1610	(.08)	430	(.02)	650
B	.5	.3	96	(.07)	6	(.01)	60	(.04)	60	(.03)	48
C	.5	.5	96	(.03)	27	(.02)	60	(.02)	172	(.03)	71
D	.75	.3	96	(.14)	99	(.12)	90	(.12)	100	(.13)	94
E	.75	.5	96	(.09)	127	(.11)	158	(.09)	140	(.13)	98
F	.75	.7	99	(.07)	172	(.04)	162	(.05)	90	(.04)	64
G	1.0	.5	99	(.19)	60	(.09)	60	(.12)	110	(.18)	76
H	1.0	.7	99	(.14)	179	(.06)	157	(.11)	70	(.09)	70
I	1.25	.5	99	(.27)	186	(.47)	147	(.38)	128	(.33)	138
Controls as % of N		11		70		64		33		50	
Total N		876		2889		2502		1300		1309	
ΣC_i (000's)		5647		1773		2296		2798		2500	
Avg. cost/obs.		6446		614		918		2152		1910	
Efficiency Relative to ANOVA (Based on ΣC_i's)		1.00		3.18		2.46		2.02		2.25	

NOTES to Table 1 appear on page 68.

no interior points when the response surface is, in fact, convex, we run the risk of overlooking a highly effective policy package represented by some intermediate combination of g and r. The sample distributed on the assumption of a planar response will show no curvature (nonlinearity) in the surface and no (or wrong) relations to the plan parameters.[10] This problem can be only partially resolved by assuming more complex response shapes in the first stage since that requires more observations at more points on the policy plane and so is more expensive, especially if the real response turns out to be linear after all. (The equal ANOVA approach is, of course, merely an extreme form of this solution which amounts to assuming a surface so complex that it is essentially estimated at each test point individually.) In short, the efficiency to be gained from making a correct prior assumption about the response shape is potentially large, but entirely dependent on outside evidence and clues as to what the probable response shape is.[11]

Experiments carried out for policy as well as scientific purposes inevitably have a number of important "secondary" objectives which involve testing for the effects of certain intervening variables and side effects of political importance. In the NJE, for example, these included testing hypotheses about the effects of payments on family stability, fertility, political and social integration, and consumption patterns which, it was asserted by some, were at least as important to resolving pragmatic political opposition to NIT as the labor supply issue. As Rees (1969) put it:

> The negative income tax proposal will have brighter prospects if our results should show that experimental families spend their payments on children's shoes more than on beer, or that experimental families participate more in elections than control families, or if experimental families stay together more than controls. Observations on families above the break-even point (who receive no payments) are of no use in answering such questions.

Notes To Table 1

SOURCES: Memo, J. Conlisk to NJ Experimenters, Feburary 1, 1969 (no title): ANOVA allocation, p. 14; No Constraints allocation, p. 15; $n_i \geqslant 20$ allocation, p. 17; Multiple Constraints allocation, p. 22; Tobin Allocation from memo, J. Tobin to H. Watts and W. Baumol, "Sample Design for NIT Experiment", May, 1969, pp. 4-11. NOTES: *Allocations in table are consolidated over four sites and three income strata. ϕB = budget share; ϕY = income-stratum share; N = total sample size; n_i = size of cell i; ΣC_i = Objective function (total cost of allocation). **Multiple Constraints: $n_i \geqslant 20$; $N \leqslant 1300$; ϕY = .3, .3, .4; control $N \geqslant 1/4$, $\leqslant 1/3$; high-g $\phi B \leqslant 1/3$.

If one provides too small a sample of actual treatment (NIT) recipients, the efficient allocation can also preclude the detection of "threshhold effects" in a number of sociological hypotheses that can only be tested with observations at all treatments. In addition, the corollary purpose of learning something about administrative costs of a potential national program is thwarted by a design which actually makes payments to so few participants.[12]

These concerns about the impact of a "pure efficiency design" on the experimental results prompted the additional model runs shown in Table 1 in which the original Watts-Conlisk allocation was modified by placing constraints on the minimum size of any cell, the maximum total sample size, the maximum share of the experimental budget that could be allocated to the control group, and the distribution of the total sample across the three income strata.[13] Column 3 displays a minimum constraint allocation in which only a minimum individual cell size is specified; the fourth column shows the allocation that results from placing a large number of constraints on the model; and the Tobin allocation is the final design chosen for the NJE.[14]

The striking feature of Table 1 is the demonstration that, in terms of the objective function costs, a number of constraints can be placed on the basic efficiency allocation without driving its cost as high as that of an equal allocation. The relative costliness of an equal (ANOVA) distribution is also reflected in the total number of observations that can be afforded under a fixed budget constraint: with no constraints (other than budget) on the pure efficiency allocation nearly three times as many observations can be had for one-third the cost of the ANOVA scheme. Constraining the allocation to a minimum cell size of twenty for each plan reduces the total sample size slightly and increases total cost about 30%, primarily by shifting control and some high payment observations into plans B and C, so that the budget share going to high income families (plan I) is somewhat reduced.[15]

If one places additional constraints on total N, the high payment budget share, the size of the control group, and the distribution by income stratum dramatically increase the average cost of an observation by shifting many more controls and a few high payment observations into plans C and G, but even this allocation is twice as efficient in terms of cost as the equal distribution. The final (Tobin) allocation is a compromise solution close to the "multiple constraints" variant, but with some ad hoc adjustments which transferred a few observations to lower cost plans. This final allocation for the NJE was further divided across four sites, three income strata, and three ethnicities as shown in Table 2. The income dimension was incorporated in the allocation model, but the possibility of differences in response by site and ethnic group was not made an integral part of the design, and this omission is responsible for a large part of the inconclusiveness of the final results.

TABLE 2
NJE Sample Allocation — Total Sample*

	Total		White		Black		Spanish Speaking Americans	
Total	1357		440		512		415	
NIT Plan:								
50–30	48	(3.5)	19	(4.3)	19	(3.8)	10	(2.4)
50–50	73	(5.4)	15	(3.4)	28	(5.6)	30	(7.2)
75–30	100	(7.4)	26	(5.9)	41	(8.1)	34	(8.2)
75–50	117	(8.6)	33	(7.5)	43	(8.6)	41	(9.9)
75–70	85	(6.3)	31	(7.0)	38	(7.6)	16	(3.9)
100–50	77	(5.7)	22	(5.0)	32	(6.4)	23	(5.5)
100–70	86	(6.3)	25	(5.7)	34	(6.8)	27	(6.5)
125–50	138	(10.2)	61	(13.9)	47	(9.4)	30	(7.2)
Controls	632	(46.6)	208	(47.2)	220	(43.8)	204	(49.2)
Site:								
Trenton	159	(11.7)	25	(5.7)	105	(20.9)	29	(7.0)
Paterson-Passaic	490	(36.1)	49	(11.1)	194	(38.6)	247	(59.5)
Jersey City	390	(28.7)	52	(11.8)	199	(39.6)	139	(33.5)
Scranton	318	(23.4)	314	(71.4)	4	(0.8)	0	(0)
Pre-Experiment Income Stratum (% of poverty line):								
0–99	414	(30.5)	119	(27.0)	139	(27.7)	156	(37.6)
100–124	454	(33.5)	153	(34.8)	173	(34.5)	128	(30.8)
125–150	489	(36.0)	168	(38.2)	190	(37.8)	131	(31.6)

SOURCE: U.S. Department of Health, Education, and Welfare, "Summary Report: New Jersey Graduated Work Incentive Experiment" (Washington: December, 1973). *The first entries in each column are the number of families; the second entries (in parentheses) are the percent of total families.

INTERPRETATION OF EXPERIMENTAL EFFECTS
FROM OPTIMAL DESIGNS

It is evident that the sample design generated by a Watts-Conlisk type model is nonorthogonal since income and other family characteristics explicitly influence the probability of a given household being assigned to a particular plan. In the NJE, interactions occur between:

(1) Preenrollment income and guarantee—Relatively high income families are more likely to be assigned to high payment plans because (a) their anticipated cost (response) is postulated by the model to decline as family income approaches its break-even point and (b) they can be expected to fluctuate back and forth across their break-even line and so not be consistent recipients of NIT payments.[16]

(2) Family income and the probability of a working wife—Because total family income (rather than just the head's income) was the criterion for enrollment, only very large families remained eligible to participate despite the earnings of a working wife, and virtually all of these were in the high income group more likely to be assigned to high payment plans. This truncation of the sample also yielded an atypical sample of working wives, those with the most tenuous connections to the labor market and inconsistent work experience.

(3) Race and plan generosity—Whites were assigned to the most generous plans with greater frequency than blacks and Spanish-speaking families. This is attributable to the staggered timing of enrollment in the four sites; the mostly black and Spanish New Jersey sites were enrolled first and the all-white Scranton sample was added nearly a year later with the result that most of the low payment plans were fully assigned from the original minority sample and the whites had to be assigned to the more generous plans to achieve the overall sample allocation specified by the model.

(4) Site and ethnicity—The pattern of residential segregation in the New Jersey cities is such that, in the central city tracts from which the NJE sample was first drawn, very few whites could be enrolled. In order to preserve racial balance in the sample, it was decided to enroll whites by adding another site, and Scranton was selected with the result that significant ethnic responses cannot be separated from site differences relating to labor markets, social milieu, and plan generosity. (The extent of site-ethnicity confounding is evident from Table 2.)

In addition, since administration of the experiment is itself a treatment—including the amount of information given to participants, the amount of checking for fraud, the handling of questions, and the like—there was an indeterminant amount of site-administrative interaction, since the NJE was administered under the same auspices, but by different field teams, in each site.

The nonorthogonal nature of the experimental design imposes some very clear constraints on the way the resulting experimental data can be analyzed since simple comparisons of group means are no longer free of stratification characteristics that interact with plan assignments and regressions must be controlled for all possible stratification variables. While nonorthogonality contributes to the efficiency with which the particular response specified in the objective function can be estimated, it reduces the efficiency with which other hypotheses can be tested.

SOME LESSONS FROM THE NJE

Without attempting an exhaustive discussion of the empirical results of the NJE,[17] one can make a number of observations about the impact of design decisions on the interpretation of the experimental results. As it happens, the two major findings that emerge with the greatest clarity from the NJE—significant ethnic differences in labor supply responses and little or no response to the tax parameter—were both unanticipated in the design process. The pitfalls include the following:

FAILURE TO INCORPORATE IMPORTANT
STRATIFICATION VARIABLES IN THE DESIGN

The most conspicuous and consistently significant experimental effect in the NJE appears in the work response by ethnic group. The dilemma may be stated in an oversimplified way as follows:

> The largest work response, and the only one consistently corresponding to theoretical expectations, was found among the *Spanish-speaking* sample who reduced their work effort about 10% over the experimental period. But this group has the smallest representation in the national population, is largely of recent immigrant status, and is especially concentrated in the urban centers of the Northeast. In short, this subsample has the least value in extrapolation of responses to the national population.

> The *black* experimental families, on the other hand, although comprising a larger share of the national population showed a marked *positive* labor supply response. That is, they increased their work effort in response to NIT payments relative to the black controls. This result runs counter to theoretical expectations and stems largely from the exceptionally bad work experience of

the black controls during the experimental period rather than from any dramatic increase in the absolute work time of black experimentals. Due to confounding of site and ethnicity and the use of "test bore" rather than nationwide sampling in the sites, it is impossible to determine whether the positive response of the blacks receiving payments reflects a real positive work response or a special ability (NIT-related?) to resist adverse shifts in local labor market conditions for blacks. Finally, the *white* subsample which represents the largest portion of the potential response to a nationwide program, especially near the sensitive break-even point, shows only a small work response over time, increasing their work effort during some quarters and decreasing it in others.

Despite the sophistication with which the total sample of 1,300 was distributed over the 8 experimental plans, in the last analysis differences among plans turned out to be far less important than differences among races, and the sample sizes in each of the ethnic subgroups were too small to detect statistically significant experimental responses to g and r at any acceptable level of precision.

This ethnic effect was confounded by site bias, since the whites in the sample were virtually all located in Scranton while the blacks and Spanish participants were located in the New Jersey sites (Jersey City, Trenton, and Paterson-Passaic), with the result that it is impossible to determine in retrospect the extent to which positive response of the blacks and negative response of the Spanish group are attributable to particular features of the metropolitan New York-New Jersey regional labor market.

Had the potential importance of ethnicity been recognized explicitly in the design process, one or both of two adjustments could have been made: (1) expansion of the total sample size to give effective subsample sizes, (2) reduction of the number of plans to be tested. Failure to incorporate an important stratification dimension in the experimental design resulted in an experiment too rich in plans and too subdivided into small samples. As Watts (n.d.: 57) expressed it, the result was:

> three separate but highly comparable sets of experimental evidence, each of which is smaller than the originally designed experiment. The precision available in each is sufficient to establish their dissimilar findings but not enough to produce a satisfying degree of confidence in the results of any of them.

DEFINING THE POLICY SPACE TOO NARROWLY

The second general finding of the NJE analyses—lack of response to the experimental parameters, particularly the tax rate—was surprising and equally frustrating since it was these individual design effects that the experiment with its range of plans was particularly designed to reveal. With regard to the apparent lack of a tax rate disincentive at least four explanations have been offered: (1) the experiment did not test widely differing tax rates—there should have been a 90% or even a 100% tax plan; (2) the nonrandom assignment of families to plans by income level had the effect of virtually excluding from the 70% tax plans all but a very few families who were actually receiving payments and so actually subject to the highest tax rate (most families assigned to the 70% plans either elected a better welfare allowance or were consistently above their break-even income); (3) the process by which observations were assigned to plans had the effect of creating cells with greater intra- than intergroup variations in effective tax differentials faced by participants so that average responses to r show no significant differences across plans (see Aaron, 1974); and (4) the awareness of individual participants of their assigned tax rate and/or their ability to calculate what it implied about the advantage of additional work effort was very low—not understanding their tax status, participants could not react in any systematic way. The first explanation suggests that the policy space was drawn too narrowly; the last suggests that a wrong set of perceived plan parameters was chosen.

Where the purpose of an experiment is to estimate a continuous response surface over a "feasible" range of plan parameters, it is not necessary and may not be desirable to limit the choice of plans to those falling within the feasible space. Indeed, where the sample allocation is designed on the basis of some expected curvature in the response surface, the more widely distributed the test plans, the better the estimate of the curvature. In the NJE case, the evidence is that the 70% tax plans, dominated by competing welfare programs at the bottom of the income scale and by high income nonrecipients at the top, were, in effect, not really tested so that the actual policy space consisted of the very narrow range between 30% to 50% r. Whether a 90% or higher tax rate would have shown any systematic impact on work effort cannot be known, of course, but it is worth noting that in negotiations between experimental designers and policy makers a decision to limit the policy space to that considered "politically possible" may amount to sacrificing one of the major reasons for experimentation. While a Watts-Conlisk type design model cannot determine the number or spacing of plans in an experimental design, it can be used to determine the cost and total required sample size of alternative layouts and to identify redundant points in a design by generating zero assignments for them.

UNPERCEIVED TREATMENT CHARACTERISTICS

While expanding the policy space implies more, or more widely spaced, plans, alternative definitions of the "treatment" may imply a reduction in the number of necessary test points. Evidence from a special survey of NJE participants conducted at the end of the experiment suggests that recipients had almost no awareness of the particular guarantee and tax rate of the plan to which they had been assigned, but had some notion of their joint effect, i.e., payments for which they were eligible.[18] The reason for the large number of plans was, of course, to test for response to variations in g and r separately, and a much larger total sample N was required than would have been necessary to test for variations in a single payments dimension. This appears to be one of the stickiest features of experimental design as there is no known method of determining in advance whether separable or joint effects will be more significant. Two adjustments to this situation are conceivable: (a) experimenters can try to make participants more aware of the plan parameters by providing them with precalculated tables, formulas, on-call personal assistance, and the like,[19] (b) some pretesting can be done to attempt to discern what aspects of the treatment are perceived by recipients. Again, there may be some tension introduced between the goals of making policy advances and increasing scientific knowledge; while economic theory postulates separate income and substitution effects for a NIT, policy-making may not require the scientific confirmation of this in order to derive assurance that labor supply reductions are not large.

NONRANDOM ATTRITION AND UNDERESTIMATED ATTRITION COSTS

Once it was determined that observations would be allocated to plans to minimize a total cost function (objective function, C, in the Watts-Conlisk model), the specification of these costs became crucial. As it happened, both administrative costs of data collection and storage and attrition costs were underestimated, but of these the attrition costs had the greater effect on the design since both the rate of attrition (initially around 50%) and, ultimately, the cost to the experiment of reducing it and following up dispersed families later to test for self-selection attrition bias proved to be large.[20] Not surprisingly, the attrition problem was especially severe among families receiving no or few payments, and these are precisely the cells to which the model assigned the largest number of observations because of their cheapness! The overall effect of underestimating attrition costs was to make the final sample allocation more uneven across treatment points than it would otherwise have been; had the real costs calculated at the end of the experiment been used instead, the sample allocation would have come closer to the kind of coverage of interior points that Rees and others had argued for earlier. It is clear that any efficient design that takes total program cost as its objective function will have to give careful attention to the bias that greater attrition in the cheap cells sets up.

TRUNCATION OF THE SAMPLE AND THE UNIT OF OBSERVATION

The criterion governing eligibility for the experimental sample has a somewhat broader impact on experimental design; by truncating the sample on a dimension linked directly to the plan parameters, one produces a nonrandom allocation of various other family characteristics to plans which may drastically constrain analysis of the final data. In the NJE case, a great deal of attention was devoted to devising a flexible and reasonably simple measure of household income to be used as the criterion for eligibility as well as the basis of the payments calculation. Questions of the optimal time period over which to measure income (a moving average system with carry-overs was adopted), the types of receipts to be included/excluded, the treatment of capital assets, and the like were fully debated, but no one thought to speculate on the truncation of the sample by race and earner that would occur by using total family income including the earnings of both husbands and wives. The result was that while the total eligible population of black families falling under the guarantee level encompassed some 60% of the total urban black population, only 20% of the white family income distribution was eligible. This in itself would not cause concern except that, when one searches the resulting data for evidence of secondary-earner response as well as natality and other consumption effects, it becomes clear that working wives have been substantially excluded from the sample by virtue of the fact that their earnings generally bring the total family income above the eligibility line.[21] The result is a very narrow and specialized sample of wives' labor supply and nonlabor responses[22] and the possibility that the responses of blacks in the sample may be more typical of their ethnic group than the responses of whites for theirs.[23] In addition, the income-plan assignment interaction mentioned previously is brought into play so that working wives are to be found heavily concentrated in high payment cells. This truncation effect is less bothersome (at least with respect to the wives' sample) if we are willing to accept the family as the unit of interest and to forego any efforts to analyze how work adjustments are made differentially within that unit. But this involves foregoing some valuable policy information (presumably we feel differently if wives or male heads cut their work effort) which could be collected at virtually no extra cost. To make this information usable at least two solutions are conceivable: (a) an increase in the total (joint) family income used to define eligibility to a level at which a "typical" sample of working wives can be obtained in the sample; (b) redefine eligibility for the experiment on the male head's income alone while using combined income to calculate payments. Other options are surely conceivable; the point is simply that nothing is simple in experimental design and even such apparently straightforward decisions as defining the unit of observation and establishing eligibility criteria are to be approached carefully, especially where a nonorthogonal efficiency design approach is being employed.

The reader who would take these observations as a condemnation of the NJE makes a great mistake. Rather, I have chosen to illustrate some abstract design points with the NJE case precisely because that experiment has not only alerted us to some pitfalls of the kind that can only be noticed by experience, but has also provided a new approach to efficient experimental design which will be indispensable to other equally expensive and complex policy experiments. The moral of the story throughout has been that efficiency comes at a price and that experimenters must think more precisely about the conditions that make that price acceptable. If there is a single lesson in the NJE design experience itself, it may be that the kinds of behavioral adjustments that can be induced and measured by the experimental process are (probably) much smaller than we are generally inclined to think and that social and aggregate labor market conditions easily swamp the individual effects of modest income and price changes. This suggests that future experiments, of necessity, will have to give careful attention to design features in order to be able to detect quite marginal responses (or nonresponse) with a convincing degree of confidence.

NOTES

1. A full-length evaluation study of the NJE is being prepared for publication under funding by the Russell Sage Foundation by Peter H. Rossi and Katharine C. Lyall.

2. In addition, the rural NIT experiments carried out in North Carolina and Iowa and the proposed RAND health insurance experiment both use variants of the Watts-Conlisk allocation process.

3. For details of how and why these particular decisions were made, see Boeckmann (1973). For more details on their impact on interpretation of the NJE results, see Lyall (1974).

4. The g-r plane at Y = 0 may be thought of as the control group response level since experimental response is measured as the experimental-control differential. The partial derivative of the response function Y(f) with respect to each of the policy parameters (g and r) defines the separate effects of guarantee and tax rate features of a NIT on earnings or hours worked by recipients.

5. In the NJE case the cheapness or expensiveness of plans is determined both by the guarantee level and the marginal tax rate—plans with high g's and low r's are more "generous" to the recipient, but more "expensive" to the budget. The NJE is further complicated by the fact that the transfer cost of any plan depends also on the earnings and work response of the recipient—precisely the magnitude that the experiment was designed to estimate in the first place.

6. Assuming an equal expected variance in each treatment cell. In the NJE case there was reason to expect unequal variances in some cells so that the ratio stipulated above would have had to have been multiplied by the ratio of control to treatment group variance for each cell assignment. The reasoning is this: since each point is treated as an independent treatment requiring its own control, the variance in the error of estimation of each response point is the sum of the variances for that point plus its controls: $\Sigma \sigma_x^2 + \sigma_y^2/k$ where k = number of design points. Under a sample size constraint, the ratio of treatment to control observations should be proportionate to the ratio of their standard deviations; under a budget constraint, the standard deviations are weighted inversely by the cost of their observations.

7. Indeed, this may be taken as a distinguishing characteristic of "experiments" which differentiates them from "demonstrations" or "pilot projects" whose focus is on establishing that a particular program (set of policy parameters) is feasible.

8. The NJE designers also tried some cubic forms for the response function, but finally rejected these as computationally cumbersome and implying a more complex response than anyone really expected to find in treatments which were relatively modest and in a policy space that was relatively narrow.

9. In the application of the design model which generated the final sample allocation for the NJE, the variances of the estimates of the response coefficients were assumed to be constant for all treatments except cells in which initial income was below g or above the break-even level. Variances for these cells were assumed to be twice as large. The final NJE design also weighted the average cost estimate for each plan by a policy weight reflecting the sponsor's judgments of the relative policy interest attaching to different plans.

10. In addition, there is some risk in concentrating observations at a few extreme points, since this will exaggerate any estimation error occurring at these points and thereby bias estimates at other points on the surface.

11. Procedures for hedging against misspecification risk have been suggested by Branson (1968), Orcutt and Orcutt (1968), Conlisk (1973), and Morris (1973). Branson suggests assigning observations under two sets of constraints, one on the acceptable probability of Type II error and the second to minimize Type I error. In practice this would mean assigning observations to each of the design points until the expected variance of the mean response at each point is reduced to some specified level and thereafter assigning the remaining observations to the most efficient points as picked out by a Watts-Conlisk model. The Orcutts suggest that a process of sequential sampling before the experimental design is set can help to reduce uncertainty about the assumed shape of Y(f). And Morris, in specifying a design for the RAND Health Insurance Experiment, proposes a sequential design in which half the sample is allocated randomly over all points, while the remaining families are assigned to specific plans by a "finite selection model," really an algorithm which scans the remaining families on the list, calculates for each one its cost effectiveness at each design point, and selects that family which will contribute the greatest reduction in variance per dollar of program cost. The advantage of this procedure is that it permits the allocation to reflect precisely the particular family characteristics (therefore, costs) of each household assigned rather than using average characteristics per plan as in the pure Watts-Conlisk formulation. Its disadvantage is that the final allocation is sensitive to the length of the screened list of participants and the refusal rate and pattern of those in the initial allocation. That is, the order in which families are drawn from the eligibility list affects their most cost-effective plan assignment. Conlisk suggests three possibilities: constraining each cell size to a minimum n_i, minimizing the expected loss calculated for each functional form versus a "true" alternative state, and placing upper and lower bounds on the amount by which estimated responses at adjacent points may differ from one another.

12. This purpose was especially important in the NIT case because a major advantage claimed for a NIT program has been that its administration could be reduced to a system of self-reporting and the mailing out of checks similar to the existing tax system, a great saving over current welfare administration costs.

13. Families were classified on the basis of their preenrollment incomes as being below the official poverty line, between 100-124%, or 125-150% above the line. Families more than 150% above the line were ineligible for enrollment.

14. So-called because James Tobin was finally asked to resolve the design controversy among the NJE experimenters who had split over the question of which of the many possible allocations should be used. For the details of the Tobin solution and how it was reached, see Rossi and Lyall (forthcoming).

15. In a recent article, Conlisk (1973) has worked out the relative efficiencies of alternative design functions and found that the greatest inefficiency arises from making an equal sample-share assignment over all points when the response is, in fact, linear, followed by using an ANOVA allocation for a linear estimate. The most efficient design is, of course, to use a linear design function to estimate a linear response.

16. Recall that the break-even line (= g/r) is the income above which the family becomes ineligible for payments. The NJE used a rather elaborate four-quarter

moving average with carry overs to calculate a family's current eligibility so that a family fluctuating above and below the break-even level might never receive payments.

17. A good summary is available in the HEW report (1973); other, more detailed, discussions can be found in the *Journal of Human Resources* (Summer 1974) and in the mimeographed final report papers of the NJE itself.

18. Knudsen et al. (n.d.) have investigated the question of information levels of participants; in general, they conclude that awareness of plan parameters was very low or nonexistent; greatest information was reported for the level of payments received.

19. Kershaw and Fair (Volume III of the Final Report of the NJE) report that participants in the NJE were told the g and r characteristics of their plan at enrollment, but were not reminded of these during the experiment. No requests were received by their field offices for further information or assistance in calculating potential effects of work adjustments.

20. The costs of data collection and storage were treated as overhead costs of the experiment and not included directly in the model's objective function so they have an impact on the total cost of the experiment to the funding agency, but not on the sample allocation directly. Tobin specified the final sample allocation on the assumption that the attrition costs of both control and experimental observations should be nearly doubled as the price for reducing maximum attrition to 20% for families receiving no payments.

21. Working wives in the NJE sample are found in large families with many children who make the family eligible, but also constitute an extraordinary claim on the wife for home work.

22. Because the wives' sample is so small and their market work commitment necessarily small, the data show large percentage adjustments by wives to the experiment, much larger than the percentage responses of their husbands. But these cannot be taken as representative of female heads or even most working wives.

23. Since the black response was countertheoretical, this is a particularly unnerving bias to have in the sample. See the statement of ethnic results previously discussed.

REFERENCES

AARON, H. (1974) "Lessons from the New Jersey-Pennsylvania income maintenance experiment." Presented at the Brookings Institution Conference, April 29-30.

BOECKMANN, M. (1973) "The contribution of social research to social policy formulation: a study of the New Jersey income maintenance experiment and the family assistance plan." Ph.D. dissertation. Johns Hopkins University.

BRANSON, W. (1968) Memo to H. Watts on "Sample selection and assignment of tax plans, continued." (May 15)

CONLISK, J. (1973) "Choice of response functional form in designing subsidy experiments." Econometrika 41, 4 (July): 643-656.

——— and M. KURZ (1972) "The assignment model of the Seattle and Denver income maintenance experiments." Stanford Research Institute Research Memorandum 15 (July).

KNUDSEN, J., J. MAMER, R. SCOTT, and A. SHORE (n.d.) "Information levels and labor response." Final Report of NJE, Section B, X.

LYALL, K. (1974) "Design issues in the New Jersey income maintenance experiment." Prepared for the Russell Sage Foundation.

METCALF, C. (n.d.) "Sample design and the use of experimental data." Final Report to OEO from NJE, Part C, ch. 5. (mimeo)

MORRIS, C. (1973) "Statistical design aspects for the health insurance study." RAND Working Paper (August).

ORCUTT, G. and A. ORCUTT (1968) "Incentive and disincentive experimentation for income maintenance policy purposes." Amer. Econ. Rev. 58 (September): 754-772.

REES, A. (1969) Memo to James Tobin: "A general view of the design model." (May 1)

RIVLIN, A. (1973) "How can experiments be more useful?" Presented at the American Economic Association meetings, December 29. (mimeo)

ROSSI, P. H. and K. C. LYALL (forthcoming) Evaluation Study of the NJE. New York: Russell Sage.

U.S. Department of Health, Education, and Welfare (1973) "Summary report: New Jersey graduated work incentive experiment." Washington, D.C. (December).

WATTS, H. (n.d.) "Labor supply response of married men." Final Report of NJE, Section B, IIa.

——— and J. CONLISK (1969) "A model for optimizing experimental design for estimating response surfaces." Presented to the Proceedings of the Social Statistics Section, American Statistical Association.

This paper addresses the question of internal validity in quasi-experimental and nonexperimental social policy research. We focus primary attention on problems of selection in research designs where assignment to experimental conditions occurs on a nonrandom basis. Five different solutions to the problems of selection are discussed—randomization, covariance adjustment, gain scores, matching, and explicit selection—and we examine the conditions under which these solutions are useful. The problem of random measurement error is discussed within the context of our elaboration of these techniques.

ISSUES OF DESIGN AND ANALYSIS
IN EVALUATION RESEARCH

DUANE F. ALWIN
Indiana University

MICHAEL J. SULLIVAN
Washington State University

*i*n recent years considerable attention has focused on the analysis of data in social policy evaluation where true experimental designs for research are either impossible or impractical. Analysts of the effectiveness of social amelioration programs frequently engage in debates over the issues involved in making policy inferences from data gathered using nonexperimental and quasi-experimental research designs (Bowles and Levin, 1968a, 1968b; Coleman, 1968, 1970; Cain and Watts, 1970; Mosteller and Moynihan, 1972; Campbell and Erlebacher, 1970a, 1970b; Cicirelli, 1970; Evans and Schiller, 1970; Pettigrew et al., 1973; Armor, 1973). The issues raised in such discussions center in large part on questions relating to the extent to which observed effects of policy variables are spuriously due to preexisting differences among treatment and control groups. Nonrandom assignment to conditions ordinarily

AUTHORS' NOTE: *The authors' work on this paper was supported in part by grants from the Washington State University Graduate School and the Public Health Services (RX-74-36-HEW). The authors thank Richard Berk and Louis Gray for reading an earlier draft of the paper. Any errors in the paper belong to the authors.*

stimulates criticism of the evaluative effort, and owing to the absence of the "definitive experiment," the policy issues are rarely, if ever, resolved. The net result is a general confusion regarding the importance of the policy variable(s) involved.

This paper addresses the question of internal validity in nonexperimental and quasi-experimental social policy research. We begin our discussion by summarizing the inferential problems involved in the analysis of observed differences among policy intervention conditions. Several sources (e.g., Campbell and Stanley, 1963; Campbell, 1969; Ross and Smith, 1968; Riecken and Boruch, 1974) present inventories of major "threats" to internal validity in experimental, quasi-experimental, and nonexperimental research settings. Among the categories cited as problematic are selection, maturation, mortality, regression to the mean, testing, instrument decay, and so on. The present treatment focuses on a limited subset of the possible alternative explanations for differences among treatment conditions. Specifically, we focus on differences among experimental conditions that may result from pretreatment differences on variables that are causally related to the criterion variable, but are not under the experimenter's control. We shall refer to such alternative explanations as *selection problems.*

We begin by developing an equational framework for the discussion of selection problems in the context of research design, with special attention to the problems of inference in nonexperimental social policy research. We show how several selection-related "threats" to internal validity discussed by Campbell (1969; see also Campbell and Stanley, 1963) and others can be treated more formally within the context of a structural equation model. Our conceptualization of the problems of inference in nonexperimental research is relatively parsimonious, and it provides a framework from which we may discuss solutions to this type of problem. Next, we discuss a set of guidelines for applying known solutions to selection problems, including both methodological and statistical/analytic solutions. We discuss the problem of measurement error within this outline of analytic strategies. We turn now to a general discussion of methodological issues relevant to the question of internal validity in evaluation research.[1]

INTERNAL VALIDITY IN EVALUATION RESEARCH

Literature on evaluation research (Suchman, 1967; Caro, 1971; Rossi and Williams, 1972; Weiss, 1972a, 1972b) is in general agreement regarding the need for rigorous research designs in the evaluation of the effectiveness of social programs aimed at social amelioration. While there is an ubiquitous viewpoint among evaluation methodologists that the optimal design for such research is the classical experimental design with randomization, it is a well-recognized fact that such designs are more often than not impractical or impossible. We think it necessary, therefore, that evaluation researchers be aware of the strengths and weaknesses of research designs that do not fit the classical experimental mold. A number of research designs involving nonrandom assignment of observations have been discussed in the methodological literature (Campbell and Stanley, 1963; Campbell, 1969). These discussions focus on the problems arising from the use of nonexperimental designs and give less attention to available solutions to the problems. The following discussion considers the solutions as well as the problems that characterize such designs.

It is useful to classify the problems involved in making inferences about the effects of policy variables in evaluation research designs into five broad categories:

(1) the problem of selection processes resulting in preintervention differences among groups, making it difficult to attribute treatment effects to observed postintervention differences;

(2) the problem of the occurrence of events unrelated to the policy intervention producing rival explanations for the effects which would otherwise be attributable to the intervention;

(3) the problem of identifying the intervening process or processes by which an observed intervention effect is actually produced;

(4) the problems of measurement error, both random and nonrandom, in variables utilized in the evaluation;

(5) the problem of differential attrition of cases due either to factors associated with selection processes, to the treatment intervention, or to postselection events unrelated to the treatment intervention.

Category 1 includes the threat to internal validity referred to as *selection* (Campbell, 1969). We point out below that when preintervention differences are measurable, this problem may be confronted using analytic (statistical) adjustments. Of course, the utility of such adjustments depends on an adequate theory regarding the relevant variables for which we should expect preintervention differences. We consider selection either to encompass or contribute to a number of other threats to internal validity. For example, the problem of maturation (main effects) as discussed by Campbell (1969) refers to a particular subclass of selection variables, namely, those associated with level of growth or development. This type of selection problem is of special relevance in the evaluation of educational programs. Also, as we point out below, the problem of *regression to the mean,* inasmuch as it is a threat to internal validity, poses problems only when preintervention differences occur on relevant selection variables. Category 1 also encompasses the selection interactions discussed by Campbell (1969; see also Campbell and Stanley, 1963).

Category 2 refers to the threats to internal validity usually discussed under the heading of *history.* Historical events, like selection processes, are in principle measurable. Therefore, they may be analytically controlled, except when they are highly associated with the policy intervention. For example, a treatment group may experience some experimentally irrelevant set of events that affect the outcome variable, while the control group does not experience such events. The main effect of history would thereby confound any inference about the effects of the treatment intervention.

Category 3 refers to a set of problems always encountered in empirical research. If the hypothesis (usually that the treatment intervention will produce a change in the criterion variable) is confirmed, we must then ask "How is this effect produced?" or "What variable or variables mediate or transmit the effect?" If the hypothesis is not confirmed, we must ask "What variable or variables dampen or inhibit the expected effect?" These problems, while they contain the most important information about the applicability of the treatment intervention to future populations, are among the most difficult to solve. Similar to problems of selection, they require the specification and measurement of omitted variables if they are to be solved.

Category 4 includes two types of measurement error. First, errors of measurement can occur as random variations in the observed scores of individuals in both pre- and postintervention measurements. This type of error can result in biases in our estimates of intervention effects in nonexperimental research designs. Second, errors of measurement can be nonrandom with respect to the true scores of individuals. For example, variation in postintervention measures which is produced by the measurement of the same or similar variables prior to any treatment intervention can be thought of as a type of nonrandom measurement error. This problem is often referred to as *testing* (Campbell, 1969). *Instrument decay* is another threat to internal validity which may be thought of in terms of measurement error. If changes in the measuring instrument do not depend on the level of the variable being measured, these changes are best thought of as random errors. By contrast, shifts which are related to the level of the measured variable are essentially nonrandom errors. When measurement error is random and some estimate of the amount of error (reliability information) is available, the problem can be corrected. The problem of nonrandom measurement error is more difficult to deal with, and few attempts have been made to remedy problems of this kind (Namboodiri et al., 1975).

Category 5 includes a set of attrition or *mortality* problems. There are no readily available solutions to such problems, although a number have been proposed (Campbell and Stanley, 1963; Campbell, 1969). If differential attrition results from selection differences on variables related to individuals' propensities to migrate out of study conditions, the problem of attrition may be viewed as a type of selection. Attrition of this type may be easily investigated, but since we usually lack information regarding the status of the dependent variable at the time of out-migration, no analytic adjustments are possible. Thus, we have no real solution to what would otherwise admit to a simple problem. When attrition results from the treatment intervention itself, the problem becomes more complicated. In such a case the attrition takes on the status of a dependent variable. Depending on the treatment under evaluation, the attrition variable may be the most important indicator of effect.

We have asserted that nonrandom assignment of observations typifies the kinds of research designs that will be available in evaluation research settings. Since these kinds of designs are especially vulnerable to selection problems, we have chosen to focus primary attention on the first category. It is our objective in the following treatment to evaluate and compare the solutions which have been suggested for the problems subsumed under that category. We consider problems associated with category 4 (measurement error) insofar as they are related to the problems and solutions involved in category 1. We begin our discussion of selection problems with a preliminary discussion of some definitions and notation.

A FRAMEWORK FOR THE DISCUSSION OF SELECTION PROBLEMS IN RESEARCH DESIGN

DEFINITIONS AND NOTATION

Suppose we have a situation in which the groups (conditions) studied are different on a number of different variables prior to any intervention of some level of the policy variable (e.g., treatment versus control groups) either by the design of the researchers or as a consequence of natural social events. Let us refer to such variables as X_k, where the index k varies over all these variables. The X_k's are referred to as selection variables. Further, let us refer to an individual's score on an X_k as X_{kij}, where the index j varies over the number of conditions included in the design and the index i varies over the number of individuals in condition j. We can conveniently represent the presence of an individual in a particular treatment condition with a binary variable Z_j which equals unity for individuals in condition j and equals zero for individuals not in condition j. We may begin with as many Z_j's as there are treatment conditions. There is by convention no Z_j for the control condition.[2] Let us refer to the criterion variables in the evaluation design as Y_p, where the index p varies over all such variables. We can represent the score of an individual on a particular criterion variable as Y_{pij}, the indexes i and j being defined as above.

A MODEL FOR THE DISCUSSION OF SELECTION PROBLEMS

We will deal for convenience with the simple case where there is a single selection variable of relevance, X_{ij}, a single criterion variable of interest, Y_{ij}, and one experimental or treatment condition, Z_j (i.e., one treatment condition and one control condition). Our conclusions regarding the operation of a single selection variable generalize to the case of multiple selection variables. Consider the following structural equation expressing the causal relationship between the criterion variable and the treatment and selection variables,

$$Y_{ij} = \beta_o + \beta_1 Z_j + \beta_2(X_{ij} - \bar{X}_{..}) + e_{ij}. \qquad [1]$$

Equation 1 states that Y_{ij} is a linear, additive function of Z_j and $(X_{ij} - \bar{X}_{.})$, plus a disturbance term, e_{ij}. The parameter β_1 is interpreted as the treatment effect. It represents the amount the criterion variable would change as a function of being in the treatment condition versus being in the control condition. The parameter β_2 is the amount Y would change as a function of a unit shift in the deviation of X from its grand mean, holding condition constant.[3]

It can be shown that the relationship between Z_j and $(X_{ij} - \bar{X}_{.})$ in equation 1 depends on the presence or absence of selection differences among the groups with respect to X_{ij}. If the population group means on X_{ij} are equivalent, the linear relationship between the two variables is reduced to zero. Conversely, if the population means are not equivalent, the relationship will not equal zero, and selection presents a potential problem in the assessment of the treatment effect. As we demonstrate formally in the next section, randomization assures the equivalence of group means in the population model for an experiment, and thus removes the selection threat to internal validity. But in the case of nonrandom assignment, selection differences pose a potential problem requiring a solution.

Nonrandom assignment can result in differences among treatment and control conditions on a large number of variables. Such differences only pose a problem if the particular selection variable is a relevant cause of the outcome measure. In equation 1 variable X_{ij} is a relevant cause of Y_{ij}. Indeed, the model states that X_{ij} is the only relevant cause of Y_{ij} other than Z_j, which is potentially related to Z_j, since by assumption the disturbance term, e_{ij}, is linearly unrelated with X_{ij} and Z_j. In equation 1 the effect of $(X_{ij} - \overline{X}_{.j})$ on Y_{ij} is β_2. If this coefficient is nonzero and the group means on X_{ij} are not equivalent, then the selection variable must be included in any equation estimating the effect of the treatment variable. This means that all relevant selection variables (defined as those which affect Y_{ij} and are correlated with Z_j) must be measured and included in the equation for Y_{ij}. By implication, then, the application of designs using nonrandom assignment places a high premium on the availability of good theoretical knowledge of the relevant selection variables.

If β_2 is nonzero this reflects the presence of the phenomenon referred to as regression to the mean, since it reflects the reality that Y_{ij} is not perfectly correlated with itself over time. This definition is consistent with discussions of the problem which emphasize the "imperfect correlation" interpretation of regression to the mean (Campbell and Clayton, 1961; Campbell and Stanley, 1963). We may therefore conclude that the problem of regression to the mean is intimately related to the problem of selection. It is ordinarily stated (e.g., Campbell and Stanley, 1963) that under the condition of randomization, regression to the mean does not present problems of inference. This is due to the fact that Z_j and $(X_{ij} - \overline{X}_{.j})$ are uncorrelated in this situation. As we demonstrate formally below, regression to the mean becomes a potential problem only when different population means exist for the experimental conditions. It becomes important, therefore, to find solutions to the problems of bias resulting from the joint operation of selection and regression to the mean. In the sections which follow we discuss five solutions which have been used to confront this problem, in the following order: randomization, covariance adjustment, use of gain scores, matching, and use of explicit selection. We discuss randomization first because it readily illustrates the nature of the problem as well as providing a methodological solution to it. In the absence of the type of methodological control utilized with randomization, one must ordinarily turn to less elegant solutions. We discuss three such solutions which have been proposed (covariance adjustment, gain scores, and matching) under the heading of "implicit selection." Finally, we discuss a second methodological approach, that of "explicit selection" in which cases are systematically assigned to treatment and control conditions on the basis of their scores on the selection variable. There are certain quasi-experimental designs, e.g., regression discontinuity analysis, which involve explicit selection.

BASIC SOLUTIONS FOR THE SIMPLE MODEL

Our later discussion will depend on and make reference to solutions to the parameters specified in equation 1. We present these here. We can derive a solution for the unknown parameters in equation 1 by first writing the normal equations.

$$\text{Cov } [Y_{ij}, Z_j] = \beta_1 \text{ Var } [Z_j] + \beta_2 \text{ Cov } [X_{ij}, Z_j] \qquad [2]$$

$$\text{Cov } [Y_{ij}, X_{ij}] = \beta_1 \text{ Cov } [X_{ij}, Z_j] + \beta_2 \text{ Var } [X_{ij}] \qquad [3]$$

By rearranging equation 2 we have

$$\beta_1 = \frac{\text{Cov } [Y_{ij}, Z_j] - \beta_2 \text{ Cov } [X_{ij}, Z_j]}{\text{Var } [Z_j]}, \qquad [4]$$

and by rearranging equation 3 we have

$$\beta_2 = \frac{\text{Cov } [Y_{ij}, X_{ij}] - \beta_1 \text{ Cov } [X_{ij}, Z_j]}{\text{Var } [X_{ij}]}. \qquad [5]$$

By substituting equation 5 for the parameter β_2 in equation 4:

$$\beta_1 = \frac{\text{Cov } [Y_{ij}, Z_j] \text{ Var } [X_{ij}] - \text{Cov } [Y_{ij}, X_{ij}] \text{ Cov } [X_{ij}, Z_j]}{\text{Var } [Z_j] \text{ Var } [X_{ij}] - \text{Cov } [X_{ij}, Z_j]^2}. \qquad [6]$$

Similarly, by substituting equation 4 for the parameter β_1 in equation 5:

$$\beta_2 = \frac{\text{Cov } [Y_{ij}, X_{ij}] \text{ Var } [Z_j] - \text{Cov } [Y_{ij}, Z_j] \text{ Cov } [X_{ij}, Z_j]}{\text{Var } [Z_j] \text{ Var } [X_{ij}] - \text{Cov } [X_{ij}, Z_j]^2}. \qquad [7]$$

EXPERIMENTS WITH RANDOM ASSIGNMENT

DEFINITION OF THE PROBLEM

It is well known that when random assignment to treatment and control conditions is a part of the research design, i.e., a true experiment (Kish, 1959; Campbell and Stanley, 1963), the covariance between X_{ij} and Z_j is set to zero in the population model for the experiment. This results from the equivalence of the expected X_{ij} means for all experimental conditions, i.e.,

$$E\,[X_{ij} | Z_j] = E\,[X_{ij}] = \overline{X}_{..} \qquad [8]$$

which is a sufficient condition for Cov $[X_{ij}, Z_j]$ being equal to zero.[4]

INTERPRETATION

A consequence of this characteristic of a true experimental design is that the solution for the treatment effect, β_1, is given by

$$\beta_1 = \text{Cov}\,[Y_{ij}, Z_j]\,/\,\text{Var}\,[Z_j] \qquad [9]$$

since Cov $[X_{ij}, Z_j] = 0$ forces the second terms in both the numerator and denominator of equation 6 to be zero and the remainder simplifies to equation 9.

It is also possible in this case to define

$$\beta_1 = \overline{Y}_{.t} - \overline{Y}_{.c} \qquad [10]$$

and

$$\beta_o = \overline{Y}_{.c} \qquad [11]$$

since (using equation 1)

$$E\,[Y_{ij} | j = t]\ = \beta_o + \beta_1\,E\,[1] \qquad [12]$$

$$\overline{Y}_{.t}\ = \beta_o + \beta_1 \qquad [13]$$

and

$$E[Y_{ij} | j = c] = \beta_o + \beta_1 E[0] \qquad [14]$$

$$\bar{Y}_{.c} = \beta_o. \qquad [15]$$

EXPERIMENTS WITH IMPLICIT SELECTION

DEFINITION OF THE PROBLEM

When random assignment to treatment and control conditions is not part of the research design, e.g., an ex post facto control group design (Campbell and Stanley, 1963), the conditions discussed for true experimental designs do not hold. In other words, in general it will be the case that $Cov[X_{ij}, Z_j] \neq 0$, which is a necessary condition for differential regression to the mean to occur. Also, in order for regression to the mean to be a problem, it is necessary that X_{ij} be a relevant cause of Y_{ij}, i.e., $\beta_2 \neq 0$. This is synonymous with saying that Y_{ij} is not perfectly correlated with itself over time (see Campbell and Clayton, 1961; Campbell and Stanley, 1963).[5]

INTERPRETATION

In the case of nonrandom assignment, i.e., where implicit selection occurs, the group means on Y_{ij} are defined as

$$E[Y_{ij} | j = t] = \beta_o + \beta_1 + \beta_2 [\bar{X}_{.t} - \bar{X}_{..}] \qquad [16]$$

$$E[Y_{ij} | j = c] = \beta_o + \beta_2 [\bar{X}_{.c} - \bar{X}_{..}] \qquad [17]$$

and

$$E[(Y_{ij} | j = t) - (Y_{ij} | j = c)] = \beta_1 + \beta_2 [\bar{X}_{.t} - \bar{X}_{.c}]. \qquad [18]$$

This leads us to an intuitively appealing solution for the treatment effect, β_1, in this case

$$\beta_1 = [\bar{Y}_{.t} - \bar{Y}_{.c}] - \beta_2 [\bar{X}_{.t} - \bar{X}_{.c}]. \qquad [19]$$

A comparison of the solutions for β_1 in equations 10 and 19 points up an interesting difference, namely, the term $\beta_2 \, [\bar{X}_{.t} - \bar{X}_{.c}]$. This term is simply the product of the linear effect of X_{ij} on Y_{ij} controlling for Z_j and the pretreatment group differences on X_{ij}. It can be shown that this term represents the differential amount of regression to the mean which occurs because of nonrandom assignment to groups, i.e., $\bar{X}_{.t} \neq \bar{X}_{.c}$.

Although we deal with the complicating problem of random measurement error, our discussion up to this point assumes perfect measurement. It should be obvious, therefore, that regression to the mean can create inferential problems stemming from pretreatment differences among groups in the absence of measurement error. The above treatment of regression to the mean is consistent with discussions of the problem which emphasize the imperfect correlation interpretation of regression to the mean (e.g., Campbell and Clayton, 1961; Campbell and Stanley, 1963). This does not mean that "measurement error" interpretations of regression to the mean are in error (see below). Our point is that the measurement error in X_{ij} is not a necessary condition for problems of interpretation arising from regression to the mean. (For a contrasting view, see Althauser and Rubin, 1971.)

Notice that the solution for β_1 in equation 19 subtracts the term representing regression to the mean from the initial $\bar{Y}_{.j}$ difference, thereby removing it from what otherwise might be viewed as the treatment effect (see equation 10). The following section deals with an array of approaches to "controlling" for selection problems in nonexperimental research designs.

ANALYTIC SOLUTIONS TO IMPLICIT SELECTION

Linear Statistical Adjustment

A general solution to problems of implicit selection which parallels the above treatment may be found in the linear statistical adjustment. Here we consider two forms of this adjustment:

(1) where there is no interaction between the policy (treatment) variable and the selection variable in their joint effects on the criterion (the classical covariance adjustment).

(2) where there is interaction between the policy (treatment) variable and the selection variable in their joint effects.

In the first instance, where the pooling of the within-group slope coefficients for the selection variable does not introduce specification error, i.e., no interaction, the adjustment is defined as

$$\bar{Y}_{.j}^* = \bar{Y}_{.j} - \sum_k \beta_{YX_k} [\bar{X}_{k.j} - \bar{X}_{k..}] \qquad [20]$$

where β_{YX_k} is in this case the common within-group slope for X_k in the regression of Y on the X_k's.

In the case discussed above the adjusted means are

$$\bar{Y}_{.t}^* = \bar{Y}_{.t} - \beta_2 [\bar{X}_{.t} - \bar{X}_{..}] \qquad [21]$$

$$\bar{Y}_{.c}^* = \bar{Y}_{.c} - \beta_2 [\bar{X}_{.c} - \bar{X}_{..}]. \qquad [22]$$

These definitions allow us to define

$$\beta_1 = \bar{Y}_{.t}^* - \bar{Y}_{.c}^* \qquad [23]$$

since by subtracting equation 22 from equation 21 and by rearranging terms we produce

$$\bar{Y}_{.t}^* - \bar{Y}_{.c}^* = [\bar{Y}_{.t} - \bar{Y}_{.c}] - \beta_2 [\bar{X}_{.t} - \bar{X}_{.c}]. \qquad [24]$$

This shows that the treatment effect defined above for the situation where nonrandom assignment to groups prevails (see equation 19) is equal to the difference between the adjusted means for the treatment and control conditions. The essential conclusion to draw from this is that the covariance adjustment is a correction for differential regression to the mean.

The second case of the linear statistical adjustment, where interaction occurs between treatment conditions and the selection variable in their effects on Y_{ij}, is somewhat more complicated. Here the adjusted means must allow for different within-group slope coefficients. Equation 20 can represent the adjustment in this situation if β_{YX_k} is defined as the within-group slope for X_k in the regression (within-group) of Y_{ij} on the X_k's. Taking the case discussed earlier and allowing for interaction, we find that the adjusted means are

$$\bar{Y}_{.t}^* = \bar{Y}_{.t} - \beta_{2t}(\bar{X}_{.t} - \bar{X}_{..}) \qquad [25]$$

and

$$\bar{Y}_{.c}^* = \bar{Y}_{.c} - \beta_{2c}(\bar{X}_{.c} - \bar{X}_{..}) \qquad [26]$$

where β_{2t} is the within treatment group slope and β_{2c} is the within control group slope.
We may now define

$$\bar{Y}^*_{.t} - \bar{Y}^*_{.c} = [\bar{Y}_{.t} - \beta_{2t}(\bar{X}_{.t} - \bar{X}_{..})] - [\bar{Y}_{.c} - \beta_{2c}(\bar{X}_{.c} - \bar{X}_{..})] \qquad [27]$$

$$= [\bar{Y}_{.t} - \bar{Y}_{.c}] - \qquad [28]$$

$$[\beta_{2t}\bar{X}_{.t} - \beta_{2c}\bar{X}_{.c} - (\beta_{2t} - \beta_{2c})\bar{X}_{..}].$$

It should be apparent that the difference between adjusted means in this case does not represent the treatment effect, β_1, as above. Indeed, it represents the treatment effect only for those persons who have scores equal to the grand mean on X_{ij}. By definition, the treatment effect differs over other levels of X_{ij}. But it is possible using this information to define the treatment effects across all levels of X_{ij}. In Figure 1 we present a hypothetical example for the case of interaction. In this example the treatment effect for a given level of X is represented by the difference between the two within-group slopes. Here the treatment effect diminishes as X increases. In general we may write the treatment effect $\beta_1 \mid X_a$ (where X_a is a particular value of X) as

$$\beta_1 \mid \bar{X}_a = [\bar{Y}_{.t} - \bar{Y}_{.c}] - [\beta_{2t}\bar{X}_{.t} - \beta_{2c}\bar{X}_{.c} - (\beta_{2t} - \beta_{2c})X_a]. \qquad [29]$$

Any statistical adjustment is only as good as the particular model employed to obtain it. It should be apparent that several fairly strong assumptions underlie this kind of statistical manipulation. An important assumption in the present two cases is that X_{ij} and Y_{ij} are linearly related. We have shown that when this assumption is met, linear statistical adjustments constitute an important solution to the problem of implicit selection, insofar as the selection process is correctly specified.

The Use of Gain Scores

It is a common practice among evaluation researchers to measure the treatment effect for individual i in condition j by computing the change which occurs as the difference between his posttreatment score and his pretreatment score on the criterion variable. While we agree in principle with Cronbach and Furby (1970: 80) that users of gain scores would be better advised to frame their questions in different ways, it is of value to discuss the use of gain scores, paying particular attention to the conditions under which they may or may not be used.

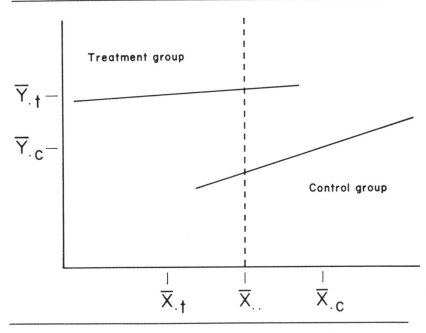

Figure 1: Hypothetical Example of Linear Adjustment with Interaction.

If in the above case X_{ij} is considered a pretreatment measurement of Y_{ij}, it is possible to compute a difference score or gain score representing the gain for individual i in condition j as

$$d_{ij} = Y_{ij} - X_{ij}. \qquad [30]$$

The following equation expresses the gain score as a function of the treatment variable plus an error term

$$d_{ij} = \beta'_o + \beta_3 Z_j + v_{ij}. \qquad [31]$$

In this equation the treatment effect is defined as

$$\beta_3 = \text{Cov} \, [d_{ij}, Z_j] / \text{Var} \, [Z_j] \qquad [32]$$

$$= [\text{Cov} \, [Y_{ij}, Z_j] - \text{Cov} \, [X_{ij}, Z_j]] / \text{Var} \, [Z_j]. \qquad [33]$$

The effect, β_3, is equivalent to the treatment effect discussed above (equation 19) only if (a) there is random assignment to treatment and control conditions (in which case equation 6 reduces to equation 9), or (b) if X_{ij} is included in the structural equation for d_{ij} above. Otherwise, the use of gain scores results in overcorrection for regression to the mean (Bereiter, 1962; Borhnstedt, 1969).

When random assignment to conditions is part of the research design, the term Cov $[X_{ij}, Z_j]$ in the numerator of equation 33 is zero in the population model for the experiment, resulting in

$$\beta_3 = \text{Cov } [Y_{ij}, Z_j] / \text{Var } [Z_j] \qquad [34]$$

which is equivalent to the solution for β_1 in equation 9.

In contrast, if random assignment to conditions is not a part of the design, β_3 is equal to β_1 only if X_{ij} is included in the structural equation for d_{ij}, as follows

$$d_{ij} = \beta_0 + \beta_3 Z_j + \beta_2 X_{ij} + e_{ij}. \qquad [35]$$

In this case $\beta_3 = \beta_1$ since

$$\beta_3 = \frac{\text{Cov } [Z_j, d_{ij}] \text{ Var } [X_{ij}] - \text{Cov } [X_{ij}, d_{ij}] \text{ Cov } [X_{ij}, Z_j]}{\text{Var } [Z_j] \text{ Var } [X_{ij}] - \text{Cov } [X_{ij}, Z_j]^2} \qquad [36]$$

and the numerator of equation 36 is

$$\text{Cov } [Z_j, Y_{ij}] \text{ Var } [X_{ij}] - \text{Cov } [Z_j, X_{ij}] \text{ Var } [X_{ij}]$$

$$- \text{Cov } [X_{ij}, Y_{ij}] \text{ Cov } [X_{ij}, Z_j] + \text{Var } [X_{ij}] \text{ Cov } [X_{ij}, Z_j] \qquad [37]$$

which simplifies to

$$\text{Cov } [Z_j, Y_{ij}] \text{ Var } [X_{ij}] - \text{Cov } [X_{ij}, Y_{ij}] \text{ Cov } [X_{ij}, Z_j] \qquad [38]$$

resulting in a solution for β_3 which is equal to the solution for β_1 in equation 6.

Summarizing the above development, if gain scores are used in policy research, we see that the design must include random assignment to conditions, or if this is not possible, the structural equation used to estimate the treatment effect must include the pretreatment measurement as a regressor. If X_{ij} is imperfectly measured, its inclusion in the equation will not adequately control for pretreatment differences in X_{ij}. This problem of measurement error is addressed below.

Matching

The problems associated with defining a control condition after the fact on the basis of matched characteristics of the treatment condition have been discussed widely (Campbell and Stanley, 1963; Campbell and Erlebacher, 1970a; Barnow, 1972; Goldberger, 1972). We briefly review the approach here. Matching can actually be used in one of three ways: (a) matching on relevant characteristics of cases prior to random assignment to treatment and control conditions, (b) matching of cases on relevant characteristics after random assignment, and (c) matching of cases to form a control group after cases have been nonrandomly assigned to the treatment condition (the case of ex post facto matching discussed above).

Case a is a generally accepted method for reducing error variance in Y_{ij} under the experimental model represented in equation 1. The rationale for this type of matching is that it increases the power of statistical tests (see Graybill, 1961). Case b is an erroneous application of the logic involved in case a, since it capitalizes on chance variation in reducing the error variance in Y_{ij} (see Graybill, 1961). Finally, considerable question has been raised regarding the utility of case c as an analytic approach to the adjustment for pretreatment differences in selection variables. Campbell and Erlebacher (1970a) illustrate how this type of matching can lead to undercorrection for regression to the mean. In short, this approach cannot be depended on as a method for analytically adjusting for pretreatment differences on relevant selection variables.

MEASUREMENT ERROR

As noted in passing earlier, random measurement error in the measurement of selection variables complicates the problem of analytically adjusting for regression to the mean. It can be shown, given equation 1 as the general model for experimental design, that where implicit selection occurs, i.e., nonrandom assignment, random measurement error on X_{ij} will attenuate the estimate of β_2. We will henceforth represent an errorful measure of X_{ij} as X'_{ij}, and we will define

$$X'_{ij} = X_{ij} + q_{ij} \tag{39}$$

$$E[q_{ij}] = 0 \tag{40}$$

$$\text{Cov } [X_{ij}, q_{ij}] = 0 \qquad [41]$$

$$\text{Cov } [Y_{ij}, q_{ij}] = \text{Cov } [Z_j, q_{ij}] = 0. \qquad [42]$$

From these assumptions it follows that (see Lord and Novick, 1968)

$$E [X'_{ij}] = E [X_{ij}] + E [q_{ij}] = E [X_{ij}] \qquad [43]$$

$$\text{Var } [X'_{ij}] = \text{Var } [X_{ij}] + \text{Var } [q_{ij}] \qquad [44]$$

$$\text{Cov } [Y_{ij}, X'_{ij}] = \text{Cov } [Y_{ij}, X_{ij}] + \text{Cov } [Y_{ij}, q_{ij}] = \text{Cov } [Y_{ij}, X_{ij}] \qquad [45]$$

$$\text{Cov } [Z_j, X'_{ij}] = \text{Cov } [Z_j, X_{ij}] + \text{Cov } [Z_j, q_{ij}] = \text{Cov } [Z_j, X_{ij}]. \qquad [46]$$

Given these results it can be seen that in equation 7 the only term in this formula affected by such error is Var $[X_{ij}]$. As a result, this term will be overestimated, and the estimate for β_2 will be attenuated. Consequently, the solution for β_1 in equation 19 will provide an overestimation of the treatment effect, or in other words, an undercorrection for regression to the mean (see Campbell and Erlebacher, 1970a).[6]

It is possible, however, that given reliability information on X'_{ij} the estimate of Var $[X_{ij}]$ can be improved. Reliability is defined as the ratio of the true variance to the observed variance (Lord and Novick, 1968), i.e., $r^2_{XX'} = \text{Var } [X_{ij}]/\text{Var } [X'_{ij}]$. It is possible, therefore, given an estimate of reliability for X'_{ij} to obtain an estimate of the true variance, Var $[X_{ij}]$, using the formula

$$r^2_{XX'} \text{ Var } [X'_{ij}] = \text{Var } [X_{ij}]. \qquad [47]$$

It is possible in theory to correct the estimate of the treatment effect, β_1, for unreliability in the measurement of X_{ij}, thereby obtaining a complete correction for regression to the mean. This solution applies to the use of gain scores discussed above as well. Obviously, one's faith in the applicability of the assumptions of classical true score theory and the veracity of the reliability information used must condition his willingness to employ this type of correction for unreliability.[7] We should point out that measurement error in Z_j, although perhaps less likely, will also complicate the estimation of the treatment effect, but we have not dealt with this here. Finally, measurement error in Y_{ij} does not affect the estimation of any of the parameters of the model—it simply produces greater variability in e_{ij} in equation 1—unless, of course, standardized parameters are estimated.

The conclusion to be drawn from this discussion is that random measurement error in X'_{ij} complicates and in most instances seriously magnifies problems existent in estimating treatment effects in research designs where implicit selection occurs. As considered here random measurement error in X'_{ij} does not affect the covariance of the variable X_{ij} with other variables (Lord and Novick, 1968: 62). However, to the extent that measurement error affects our estimate of the linear effect of X_{ij} on Y_{ij} we obtain a biased estimate of the amount of regression to the mean, resulting in a biased estimate of the treatment effect, unless we can correct for unreliability in X'_{ij}. In the following section we consider a case in which we do not assume Cov $[Z_j, q_{ij}]$ = 0, but it is possible to obtain an unbiased estimate of the treatment effect using a method called explicit selection.

EXPERIMENTS WITH EXPLICIT SELECTION

DEFINITION OF THE PROBLEM

Up to this point our discussion has taken the conventional point of view that if selection variables affect Y_k, the optimal design for policy research is one incorporating random assignment of cases to treatment and control conditions. We have taken the position as well that when random assignment to conditions is prohibited, selection variables producing pretreatment differences among groups can result in biases in the estimation of treatment effects. We have pointed out, however, that in such cases the bias (i.e., differential regression to the mean) which results can under appropriate conditions be "adjusted for" analytically. We have reviewed some analytic techniques for doing so, and we have evaluated the conditions under which they are useful.

At this point we shall shift our attention to a less conventional method—that of explicit selection. Explicit selection occurs when cases are assigned to treatment and control conditions as a function of their observed scores on a selection variable, X_k. There are a number of research designs in which assignment to groups is explicitly nonrandom, e.g., "regression discontinuity analysis" (Campbell and Stanley, 1963; Campbell, 1969). The distinction between "observed" scores and "true" scores is important here, since ordinarily one does not have perfect measurement of X_k. We will refer to the observed score on X_k (as above) as X_k'. Goldberger (1972) has shown that when an X_k (a perfectly measured selection variable) is used to nonrandomly assign cases to treatment and control conditions, bias will result in the estimate of the treatment effect unless the value of X_k is controlled analytically, e.g., using the covariance adjustment. However, Goldberger also shows that if assignment takes place on the basis of X_k' (an imperfectly measured selection variable), and certain other conditions hold, an unbiased estimate of the treatment effect can be obtained.[8] The following discussion develops Goldberger's argument within the context of the present analytic and notational scheme.

Assume the situation where, not only is there an equation for Y_{ij} (as in equation 1 above), but also there is an equation for Z_j as well, of the form

$$Z_j = \beta_o' + \beta_3 X_{ij}' + \beta_4 X_{ij} \qquad [48]$$

where X_{ij}' is defined as above (in the section on measurement error), and where it is assumed that $\beta_4 = 0$, i.e., that assignment to condition Z_j is on the basis of X_{ij}', not X_{ij}.

As a result of these assumptions we can solve for β_3 by first writing the normal equation

$$\text{Cov } [Z_j, X_{ij}'] = \beta_3 \text{ Var } [X_{ij}'] \qquad [49]$$

and by rearranging it algebraically, producing

$$\beta_3 = \text{Cov } [Z_j, X_{ij}'] / \text{Var } [X_{ij}']. \qquad [50]$$

We can also write the normal equation

$$\text{Cov } [Z_j, X_{ij}] = \beta_3 \text{ Cov } [X_{ij}', X_{ij}] \qquad [51]$$

$$= \beta_3 \text{ Var } [X_{ij}]. \qquad [52]$$

Substituting the solution for β_3 in equation 50 into equation 52 results in

$$\text{Cov } [Z_j, X_{ij}] = \text{Cov } [Z_j, X_{ij}'] \text{ Var } [X_{ij}] / \text{Var } [X_{ij}'] \qquad [53]$$

$$= \text{Cov } [Z_j, X_{ij}'] \, \alpha_{x_{ij}} \qquad [54]$$

where $\alpha_{X_{ij}} = r^2_{XX'}$ is defined in the section on measurement error. Finally, we may write the normal equations for Cov $[Y_{ij},Z_j]$ and Cov $[Y_{ij},X_{ij}]$ contained in equations 2 and 3. Substituting equation 54 into equations 2 and 3 results in

$$\text{Cov } [Y_{ij},Z_j] = \beta_1 \text{ Var } [Z_j] + \beta_2 \text{ Cov } [Z_j,X'_{ij}] \; \alpha_{X_{ij}} \qquad [55]$$

$$\text{Cov } [Y_{ij},X_{ij}] = \beta_1 \text{ Cov } [Z_j,X'_{ij}] \; \alpha_{X_{ij}} + \beta_2 \text{ Var } [X_{ij}]. \qquad [56]$$

INTERPRETATION

As a consequence of the above development, we can solve for β_1 by first obtaining (from equation 56 above)

$$\beta_2 = \frac{\text{Cov } [Y_{ij},X_{ij}] - \beta_1 \text{ Cov } [Z_j,X'_{ij}] \; \alpha_{X_{ij}}}{\text{Var } [X_{ij}]} \qquad [57]$$

and the substitution of this result for β_2 into equation 55 produces

$$\text{Cov } [Y_{ij},Z_j] = \beta_1 \text{ Var } [Z_j] +$$

$$\left[\frac{\text{Cov } [Y_{ij},X_{ij}] - \beta_1 \text{ Cov } [Z_j,X'_{ij}] \; \alpha_{X_{ij}}}{\text{Var } [X_{ij}]} \right] \left[\text{Cov } [Z_j,X'_{ij}] \; \alpha_{X_{ij}} \right]. \qquad [58]$$

By manipulating equation 58 we arrive at the solution for β_1 as

$$\beta_1 = \frac{\text{Cov } [Y_{ij},Z_j] \text{ Var } [X_{ij}] - \text{Cov } [Y_{ij},X_{ij}] \text{ Cov } [Z_j,X'_{ij}] \; \alpha_{X_{ij}}}{\text{Var } [Z_j] \text{ Var } [X_{ij}] - \text{Cov } [Z_j,X'_{ij}]^2 \; \alpha^2_{X_{ij}}} \qquad [59]$$

Since it is apparent in equation 54 that Cov $[Z_j,X_{ij}]$ = Cov $[Z_j,X'_{ij}] \; \alpha_{X_{ij}}$ the solution for β_1 reduces to equation 6.

The importance of the above demonstration should perhaps be emphasized. It allows the researcher to nonrandomly assign cases to treatment and control conditions when random assignment is either impossible or impractical, yet it allows an unbiased estimate of the treatment effect to be obtained. The method will obviously not apply in situations where implicit selection occurs, e.g., ex post facto designs.

SUMMARY AND CONCLUSION

Insofar as they exist, problems of selection constitute a major stumbling block to sound empirical evaluation research in quasi-experimental and nonexperimental research settings. There is general consensus among policy researchers that evaluation of social programs is ineffectual in the absence of comparison groups. The principal inferential device whereby the effects of various policies are made known involves the incorporation of valid comparison into research designs aimed at evaluation. Because evaluation research is often characterized by designs involving comparisons among nonequivalent treatment and control groups, preintervention (selection) differences must be taken into account.

In the above presentation we have developed a formal statement of the problems inherent in quasi- and nonexperimental research, and we have reviewed the available methodological and analytic solutions to these problems. We discuss five solutions which have been used in the evaluation research literature and evaluate the conditions under which they are useful. As the classical model for the control of preexperimental differences, randomization is highly regarded as the most elegant (efficient and uncomplicated) method of ruling out alternative explanations involving selection. Where it is possible researchers should seek to employ this method. Recognizing that this approach is often unavailable to evaluation researchers for reasons of ethics and/or practicalities, we emphasize the need for evaluators to be familiar with research designs utilizing other methods for ruling out selection hypotheses.

If the researcher has control over the allocation of observations to experimental conditions, but is precluded from the use of randomization, it is possible to assign observations to treatment and control conditions as an exact function of their observed scores on a selection variable. This method, although it is rarely used, produces, with somewhat less efficiency, the same amount of control as that offered by randomization. In other words, unbiased estimation of treatment effects is possible using this method.

Finally, when the allocation of observations to experimental conditions is not under the control of the researcher, he must rely on naturally occurring treatment and control groups ex post facto. Given the likelihood of self-selection and the implicit operation of other selection processes, the reality of selection differences among conditions must be approached analytically. Traditionally, techniques such as matching and gain scores have received considerable use. However, their simplicity is essentially misleading, and their use can lead to inferential errors of unknown quantity. It is our conclusion that where the assumption of linearity is appropriate, the linear statistical adjustment is the best analytic approach to the control of preintervention selection differences among experimental conditions.

NOTES

1. Since writing this paper we have discovered two very recent articles in the literature which discuss some of these same issues. The reader may find these useful: Porter and Chibucos (1975) and Kenny (1975).

2. We assume most research designs include at least one treatment condition and one control condition.

3. We have stated that this model assumes linearity and additivity. In the latter case we assume therefore that the treatment effect is the same regardless of individuals' scores on X_{ij}, and the effect of the selection variable is constant over all treatment and control conditions. This latter parameter is invariant regardless of whether we treat X_{ij} as deviated from its grand mean. The rationale for expressing X_{ij} in deviated form involves the interpretation of β_0 and β_1 in equation 1. This is discussed in greater detail below. In addition, our discussion assumes bivariate normality for X and Y within treatment and control conditions. In our presentation we have followed a conventional dummy variable regression logic in representing the treatment and control conditions (see Cohen, 1968). Other approaches are possible (e.g., see Namboodiri et al., 1975).

4. The proof of this is straightforward, since

$$\text{Cov}\,[X_{ij},Z_j] = \text{Cov}\,[\bar{X}_{.j},Z_j] + \text{Cov}\,[X_{ij} - \bar{X}_{.j},Z_j]$$

$$= \text{Cov}\,[\bar{X}_{..},Z_j] + \text{Cov}\,[X_{ij} - \bar{X}_{..},Z_j].$$

The first term on the right side of the equation is zero since $\bar{X}_{..}$ is a constant; the second term is zero since Z_j is a constant within groups.

5. If there were perfect auto-correlation for Y_{ij} over time, there would be no room for causation of Y_{ij} from other sources.

6. In the general multivariate case (multiple X_k's) we cannot easily predict the direction of bias in the treatment effect due to random measurement error.

7. Another solution to the problem of measurement error in experimental data using multiple indicators is discussed by Alwin and Tessler (1974).

8. Goldberger also shows that while the estimate is unbiased, it will not be efficient.

REFERENCES

ALTHAUSER, R. P. and D. RUBIN (1971) "Measurement error and regression to the mean in matched samples." Social Forces 50 (December): 206-214.

ALWIN, D. F. and R. C. TESSLER (1974) "Causal models, unobserved variables, and experimental data." Amer. J. of Sociology 80 (July): 58-86.

ARMOR, D. (1973) "The double standard: a reply." Public Interest 30 (Winter): 119-131.

BARNOW, B. S. (1972) "Conditions for the presence or absence of a bias in treatment effect: some statistical models for Head Start evaluation." Discussion Paper 122-72. Institute for Research on Poverty. University of Wisconsin, Madison.

BEREITER, C. (1962) "Some persisting dilemmas in the measurement of change," in C. W. Harris (ed.) Problems in the Measurement of Change. Madison: Univ. of Wisconsin Press.

BOHRNSTEDT, G. W. (1969) "Observations on the measurement of change," pp. 113-133 in E. F. Borgatta and G. W. Bohrnstedt (eds.) Sociological Methodology 1969. San Francisco: Jossey-Bass.

BOWLES, S. and H. M. LEVIN (1968a) "More on multicollinearity and the effectiveness of schools." J. of Human Resources 3 (Spring): 393-400.

––– (1968b) "The determinants of scholastic achievement—an appraisal of some recent evidence." J. of Human Resources 3 (Winter): 3-24.

CAIN, G. C. and H. W. WATTS (1970) "Problems in making policy inferences from the Coleman Report." Amer. Soc. Rev. 35 (April): 228-242.

CAMPBELL, D. T. (1969) "Reforms as experiments." Amer. Psychologist 24 (April): 409-429.

––– and K. N. CLAYTON (1961) "Avoiding regression effects in panel studies of communication impact." Studies in Public Communication 3 (Summer): 99-118.

CAMPBELL, D. T. and A. ERLEBACHER (1970a) "How regression artifacts in quasi-experimental evaluations can mistakenly make compensatory education look harmful," pp. 185-210 in J. Hellmuth (ed.) Disadvantaged Child. Vol. 3. New York: Brunner/Mazel.

––– (1970b) "Reply to the replies," pp. 221-225 in J. Hellmuth (ed.) Disadvantaged Child. Vol. 3. New York: Brunner/Mazel.

CAMPBELL, D. T. and J. STANLEY (1963) "Experimental and quasi-experimental designs for research on teaching," pp. 171-247 in N. Gage (ed.) Handbook for Research on Teaching. Chicago: Rand McNally.

CARO, F. G. (1971) Readings in Evaluation Research. New York: Russell Sage.

CICIRELLI, V. G. (1970) "The relevance of the regression to the mean artifact problem to the Westinghouse-Ohio evaluation of Head Start: a reply to Campbell and Erlebacher," pp. 211-215 in J. Hellmuth (ed.) Disadvantaged Child. Vol. 3. New York: Brunner/Mazel.

COHEN, J. (1968) "Multiple regression as a general data-analytic system." Psych. Bull. 70 (December): 426-443.

COLEMAN, J. S. (1970) "Reply to Cain and Watts." Amer. Soc. Rev. 35 (April): 242-249.

––– (1968) "Equality of educational opportunity: reply to Bowles and Levin." J. of Human Resources 3 (Spring): 237-246.

CRONBACH, L. J. and L. FURBY (1970) "How should we measure 'change'—or should we?" Psych. Bull. 74 (July): 68-80.

EVANS, J. W. and J. SCHILLER (1970) "How preoccupation with possible regression artifacts can lead to a faulty strategy for the evaluation of social action programs: a reply to Campbell and Erlebacher," pp. 216-220 in J. Hellmuth (ed.) Disadvantaged Child. Vol. 3. New York: Brunner/Mazel.

GOLDBERGER, A. S. (1972) "Selection bias in evaluating treatment effects: some formal illustrations." Discussion Paper 123-72. Institute for Research on Poverty. University of Wisconsin, Madison.

GRAYBILL, F. A. (1961) An Introduction to Linear Statistical Models. Vol. 1. New York: McGraw-Hill.

KENNY, D. (1975) "A quasi-experimental approach to assessing treatment effects in the nonequivalent control group design." Psych. Bull. 82 (May): 345-362.

KISH, L. (1959) "Some statistical problems in research design." Amer. Soc. Rev. 24 (June): 328-338.

LORD, F. M. and M. R. NOVICK (1968) Statistical Theories of Mental Test Scores. Reading, Mass.: Addison-Wesley.

MOSTELLER, F. and D. P. MOYNIHAN (1972) On Equality of Educational Opportunity. New York: Random House.

NAMBOODIRI, N. K., L. F. CARTER, and H. M. BLALOCK, Jr. (1975) Applied Multivariate Analysis and Experimental Designs. New York: McGraw-Hill.

PETTIGREW, T. F., E. L. USEEM, C. NORMAND, and M. S. SMITH (1973) "Busing: a review of 'the evidence'." Public Interest 30 (Winter): 88-118.

PORTER, A. C. and T. R. CHIBUCOS (1975) "Common problems of design and analysis in evaluative research." Soc. Methods and Research 3 (February): 235-257.

RIECKEN, H. W. and R. F. BORUCH (1974) Social Experimentation: A Method for Planning and Evaluating Social Intervention. New York: Academic Press.

ROSS, J. and P. SMITH (1968) "Orthodox experimental designs," pp. 333-389 in H. M. Blalock, Jr. and A. B. Blalock (eds.) Methodology in Social Research. New York: McGraw-Hill.

ROSSI, P. H. and W. WILLIAMS (1972) Evaluating Social Programs. New York: Seminar Press.

SUCHMAN, E. A. (1967) Evaluative Research. New York: Russell Sage.

WEISS, C. H. (1972a) Evaluation Research: Methods of Assessing Program Effectiveness. Englewood Cliffs, N.J.: Prentice-Hall.

——— (1972b) Evaluating Action Programs: Readings in Social Action and Education. Boston: Allyn & Bacon.

This paper delimits and explicates threats to external validity particularly problematic in evaluation research. Five categories of factors are discussed: selection effects, measurement effects, confounded treatment effects, situational effects, and effects due to differential mortality. The paper focuses on pointing up specific ways in which each of the factors threaten generalizability and possible solutions to the methodological problems presented.

EXTERNAL VALIDITY AND
EVALUATION RESEARCH

A Codification of Problems

ILENE N. BERNSTEIN
Indiana University

GEORGE W. BOHRNSTEDT
Indiana University

EDGAR F. BORGATTA
Queens College
City University of New York

*e*valuative research is the application of scientific methods to the problem of assessing the effectiveness of an activity (or program) in attaining a desired goal. In the last decade there has been an increasing interest in evaluative research as a handmaiden to social policy (Weiss, 1970). It is thought that the results of evaluation research can provide a rational basis for decisions either to modify, terminate, or expand the ever-growing number of social action programs competing for public support.

Despite the commitment to and interest in furthering the development of evaluation research, the applications remain seriously wanting. Bern-

AUTHORS' NOTE: *An earlier version of this paper was presented at 1974 Conference on Evaluation Research Methodology, American Sociological Association Methodology Section, Loyola University, Chicago, Illinois. The authors are grateful for comments on the earlier draft by Dale Blyth, Robert F. Boruch, Peter J. Burke, Martin R. Frankel, and Sheldon Stryker. Author order is according to foot size.*

stein and Freeman (1975), in a review of the methodological procedures used by federally funded evaluation researchers in fiscal 1970, concluded that the problem was not so much a lack of available methodological techniques as it was the lack of use of those techniques available. In examining the self-reported responses of 236 evaluation researchers, they found, for example: (1) only 25% of the researchers report their study made use of an experimental OR quasi-experimental design with randomization and a control or comparison group; (2) only 59% selected the sample population to be studied on a random basis; (3) only 50% observed a sample representative of the larger population to which they wish to generalize; and (4) only 35% characterized their research as largely quantitative. Clearly, the inference to be drawn is that evaluation research is lacking in the application of appropriate research designs, sampling procedures, and data analytic techniques. More specifically, much evaluation research seems to be plagued by serious problems in research design, making dissemination and utilization of its results problematic if not useless.

Campbell and Stanley (1963) distinguished problems of internal validity from those of external validity for various research designs. Internal validity refers to the degree to which a design allows one to rule out alternative explanations for the way in which a particular independent variable is causally related to the dependent variable of interest. By contrast, external validity refers to the degree of generalizability from one's study to some larger, hypothetical population of interest. While problems of internal validity are as important as problems of external validity (indeed, any threat to internal validity must also logically threaten external validity), this paper concentrates on external validity only, since it is our observation that this topic has received considerably less attention by evaluation research methodologists than have problems of internal validity. As long as evaluation research purports to function as a handmaiden to policy, it is essential that the results of such studies be valid for a variety of intended target populations in varied locales with varied staffs and varied subjects. This is especially true with the advent of national program experiments such as the Negative Income Tax Experiments and the Head Start Program. Resources are just not available to evaluate every action program and project currently under way. If the worth of evaluation research is to be recognized, care needs to be taken to ensure that the results of evaluation studies undertaken provide maximum utility for policy decisions, i.e., they need be as externally valid as possible.

Campbell and Stanley (1963) provided a checklist of factors that might threaten internal and external validity, and Bracht and Glass (1968) provided a more detailed list of factors that might threaten external validity. Delimited below is a list of factors that are specifically germane to evaluation, in that they may threaten the external validity of evaluation research findings. While neither exhaustive nor mutually independent, the factors are grouped into five categories: *selection effects, measurement effects, confounded treatment effects, situational effects,* and *effects due to differential mortality.*

SELECTION EFFECTS

Two major purposes of research are (1) to estimate the effects a set of treatments has on some prespecified set of dependent variables, and (2) to generalize these estimates from the sample studied to some larger target population. Unfortunately, the populations to which evaluation researchers wish to generalize often cannot be easily enumerated, or the expense of doing so would be prohibitive. Therefore, it often is not feasible to draw a probability sample of elements from the target population. Instead, the researcher must sometimes be content with a biased selection of observations, which means that to some extent, external validity will suffer. Four types of such selection biases are listed below, in order of the degree to which they threaten external validity.

SELF-SELECTION OF RESPONDENTS INTO TREATMENT AND CONTROL CONDITIONS

Obviously, if clients themselves determine whether or not to seek treatment, one never knows whether it is the treatment itself which is responsible for observed differences between the experimental and control groups, or whether other variables correlated with the selection of treatment versus control are responsible for the observed effects. While random assignment to experimental and control groups is the optimal procedure to follow, Rossi (1972) points out that many social action programs, once put into effect, are available on a self-selection basis to a larger client population. In this case the target population can be defined as including only those motivated to seek participation in a particular program. Specifically, one might randomly assign subjects to different treatment conditions and evaluate which is the most effective *for those persons seeking treatment.* For example, persons seeking marital counseling might be randomly assigned to group versus individual counseling; the researcher would then be justified in concluding that for those who sought counseling, one method of therapy is superior. However, generalizing to some larger population of persons motivated to seek counseling would assume that this particular sample of counselees represents the larger target population (i.e., all persons seeking counseling). Without random sampling from this larger population, the degree of external validity is unknown. Quite obviously, if one found that one type of counseling improved marital relations for those seeking counseling, it could be a serious error to generalize that all couples having marital difficulties should seek counseling. Similarly, one could be in serious error in concluding that a campaign should be mounted to get persons with difficulties to volunteer for a program of counseling since this population would not be the same as the original set of volunteers.

In some cases, the use of samples of accessible persons is justifiable even though large-scale experimentation is not feasible, i.e., when one can devise control groups from subjects motivated to participate. For example, if a given Job Corps training program has a limited number of slots available and an excess of applicants, an excellent naturally occurring control group exists, composed of those who sought entrance into the program, but could not be accommodated, assuming entrance is barred by chance alone.

To reiterate, whenever subjects self-select themselves into the treatment conditions, both internal and external validity are jeopardized. However, for programs in which it is anticipated that only volunteers will seek treatment, it is possible to design research from which reasonable generalizations for that target population can be drawn.

SELECTION BY EXCELLENCE

Observational units are chosen because of presumed likelihood of demonstrating the hypothesized effects.

A common practice in evaluation research is the evaluation of programs selected because of their assumed excellence. The logic of this procedure is that such programs are the ones most likely to generate positive results. Therefore, observing them may reveal such factors as: how best to administer the program, what type of staff is conducive to program effectiveness, and what particular program components seem to precipitate the greatest positive effects. However, the problem with such a selection procedure lies in drawing inferences from the results. If one is comparing excellent programs with nonexcellent programs, the specific program inputs which are causally related to the attainment of program outputs must be delimited in detail such that they can be replicated. Cain and Hollister (1972: 118) refer to this as the replicability criterion:

It is sometimes argued by administrators that evaluations which are based upon samples drawn from any centers of a program are not legitimate tests of the program concept since they do not adequately take into account the differences in the details of individual projects or of differentiated populations. These attitudes frequently lead the administrators or other champions of the program to select, either *ex ante* or *ex post,* particular "pet" projects for evaluations that "really count." In the extreme, this approach consists of looking at the successful programs (based on observations of ongoing or even completed programs) and then claiming that these are really the ones that should be the basis for the evaluation of the program as a whole. *If* these successful programs have worked with representative participants in representative surroundings and *if* the techniques used—including the quality of the administrative and operational personnel—can be replicated on a nationwide basis, *then* it makes sense to say that the evaluation of the particular program can stand for an evaluation of the overall program. But we can seldom assume these conditional statements. After all, each of the individual programs, a few political plums notwithstanding, was set up because someone thought it was worthwhile.

Quite obviously, then, generalizable conclusions on program effectiveness cannot ordinarily be drawn when units are chosen on the basis of their presumed excellence. The assumption that one can replicate the staff, monitoring procedures, and so on in other locations is dubious at best. There is one exception to this situation. If it is indeed the case that (a) one has randomly chosen units in which the staff has followed the program guidelines to the letter, and (b) the clients served are representative of the target population, and (c) the researcher finds that under these optimal conditions the program has no effect, then it would seem safe to conclude that the program also would have no effect under less optimal conditions. However, this is a highly restrictive set of conditions.

SELECTION BY EXPEDIENCE

Observational units are chosen solely because of availability.

Bernstein and Freeman (1975: ch. 4) cite the case of an evaluator who selected his sample for the evaluation study on the basis of "persons available and willing to talk." Such a procedure can be titled selection by expedience.

Ideally, in the best of all possible worlds, the evaluator would draw a random sample of persons, centers, or programs, from the population to which he or she wished to generalize. Except for a few large-scale programs, random samples of this sort are not usually feasible. Most action programs are operationalized in only one or a few locations. For example, income maintenance experiments are being carried out in New Jersey, Gary, Seattle, and Denver, and even these experiments vary somewhat from each other in the eligibility requirements for participation. Does the lack of a random sample of the nation's poor mean that inference from these experiments is impossible? Technically speaking, yes; practically speaking, no. If one has no reason to believe that the poor of New Jersey differ significantly from the poor of Los Angeles, then one can make a tentative generalization about the poor of Los Angeles, even though no one from Los Angeles was sampled. Such inferences will be erroneous to the degree that the poor in different areas differ in ways that interact with the treatment. However, simply because one does not have a random sample of the population to which he/she ultimately wishes to generalize does not mean generalizations should not be made. Cornfield and Tukey (1956) argued strongly for this position. They characterized inference as being a bridge with two spans linked by an island: an inference from one's observations to some population (even if it is not specific); and an inference from that population to some larger group of observations. They termed the first span the "statistical span"; the second, the "subject-matter span." For example, an evaluation researcher studying a random sample of welfare recipients participating in the Work Incentive Program (WIN) in 1968 in the Minneapolis-St. Paul metropolitan area, strictly speaking, can only generalize to that area during that time period (the statistical span); but, in fact, he/she and the agency also want to generalize to all welfare recipients in all parts of the country for all years after 1968 (the subject-matter span). Both types of generalizations are important. And in particular, when the subject-matter span is weak, i.e., when there is little knowledge as in the case with most programs, it makes sense to move the island closer to the subject-matter share, even though the statistical span is weaker as a result.

Some caveats are appropriate here. First, it is necessary to stress the tentative nature of any inferences, random sample or not. Thus, generalizations from nonrandom samples must be drawn much more cautiously; second, replication always increases one's confidence in a set of findings. While the replication of results in a new sample from the *same* population increases one's confidence in the results, replication with samples from *different* populations provides even greater evidence for the original set of findings. For example, if cash transfers do not affect the incentive to work in New Jersey, and this finding is replicated in Gary, Denver, and Seattle, our confidence in this finding would increase greatly even though these cities were not randomly chosen. The fact that the programs have different eligibility criteria would strengthen our confidence in the finding even further, were it replicated in each experiment. Confidence in both positive and negative findings increases with this type of replication.

Problems occur when findings do not replicate from sample to sample. If samples are not random, it is possible that differences are due to systematic differences in the samples, or more precisely there is a sample-treatment interaction effect. If accessibility is thought to be related to variables that interact with the treatment, then problems in external validity seem certain and such samples should be avoided. To illustrate, if one has reason to believe that only agencies, schools, or centers with a history of innovation are volunteering, one should be extremely cautious in making generalizations to other observational units. Obviously, the better the case an evaluator can make (from census data, school records, agency files, and so on) that a nonrandom sample is not systematically different from the target population, the more confidence one can have in the external validity of one's findings.

NONRANDOM POSTTREATMENT MATCHING

Very often the evaluation researcher is called in to evaluate programs after the programs have been in effect for some time. Furthermore, often such programs do not include or provide for control or comparison groups. Thus, the researcher is faced with the seemingly impossible task of trying to draw conclusions about a program in the absence of a basis for comparison. A common technique is to pair each "experimental" subject with a selected "control" subject matched on variables which are assumed to be correlated with the dependent variable(s) of interest, in an attempt to estimate the independent effects of the action program. While the notion that "some control group is better than no control group" may be a truism, matching is a very poor substitute for randomization. First, when randomization is employed, the expected relationship between the potentially confounding variables is zero as is the relationship of each to the dependent variable(s). But in a nonexperimental research situation it normally is not the case that potentially confounding variables are uncorrelated with each other. Furthermore, if one tries to match subjects on more than three or four variables, often it is very difficult to find matches. Indeed, as the number of variables for matching increases, experience indicates that the control group may be a highly idiosyncratic sample of the population from which it was drawn.

Thus while matching would seem to be a reasonable alternative to randomization, in practice, for most cases, it turns out to be a very poor substitute. As such, it becomes clear that the action and evaluation components must be done contemporaneously in order to avoid the use of designs that hamper the ability to draw valid conclusions about program effects.

To summarize, we have touched on how selection effects can jeopardize external validity in evaluation research. Under this heading four types of selection types were enumerated. The general conclusions are: (1) selection effects can seriously affect generalizability; (2) even in cases where selection factors are at play it may be possible to devise designs which allow for valid conclusions to be drawn; (3) even though the samples utilized are not random samples of the target population, generalizations may still be warranted when replications are made; and (4) many problems posed by selection biases could be avoided if the evaluation aspects of a given study are simultaneously designed with the design of the action program.

MEASUREMENT EFFECTS

The term "measurement effects" is used very broadly here to include effects due to (a) the unreliability and invalidity of measurement, (b) what Campbell and Stanley (1963) term the "reactivity" of some measures, and (c) interactions between measurement and other variables.

MEASUREMENT ERROR

Measurement error jeopardizes both internal and external validity. As is well known, when one uses unreliable measuring instruments (Lord and Novick, 1968), estimated relationships are biased, usually attenuating the relationships. In effect this means that when measurement error is present, generalization of effects will commonly be conservative. While underestimates are generally more desirable than overestimates, it is clear that in evaluation research settings, underestimates can result either in termination of the action program because of presumed small effects, or an inflated cost-benefit estimate.

The solution to the problem of measurement error is not an easy one since few measures in the social and social psychological domains have high reliabilities. However, since it is known that estimates of effect are biased when measurement error exists, the evaluation researcher should (1) choose or design measures that have demonstrated high reliability, and (2) correct estimates obtained for unreliability in order to get an estimate of the true relationships.

It is sometimes argued that certain phenomena of interest to the policy maker simply are not quantifiable, or that the available measures do not capture the subtleties or complexity of the phenomenon. Certainly, some variables are more difficult to measure than are others, but if program effects are presumed to exist, they must be demonstrable. To suggest that one cannot measure some presumed effect is tantamount to saying that it belongs in a class of extraempirical variables. Such a position is clearly antiscientific since it does not allow for the falsifiability of one's hypotheses.

PRETEST SENSITIZATION

Pretest sensitization refers to the possibility that the administration of a pretest in and of itself might affect experimental results. For example, measuring public attitudes toward ex-convicts prior to an action program aimed at changing the public's view of ex-convicts may sensitize the sample to respond to the program in a way different than a nonpretested sample. Thus generalizations would hold only for pretested populations.

Campbell (1957) and Campbell and Stanley (1963) considered pretest sensitization a sufficiently serious threat to internal and external validity such that they made a strong argument for using a posttest-only design (with randomization) rather than the traditional pretest-posttest design with randomization. However, in a more recent publication, Campbell (1969) withdrew considerably from this position. A series of experiments by Lana and associates (see Lana, 1969) indicated that, across a wide variety of opinions and attitudes, either (1) there was no difference in experimental effects between pretested and posttested groups, or (2) where differences were found, it was shown that smaller changes occurred for the pretested than for the posttested groups—that is, if anything pretested tended to result in under- rather than overestimates of effects. Based on these findings Campbell concluded that while pretest sensitization may logically jeopardize internal and external validity, the experimental evidence thus far suggests that the actual effects are small. These results suggest that no easy rule of thumb exists to indicate whether the researcher should use a pretest design or not, where generalizations will be to nonpretested populations. The costs of using a posttest-only design are (1) uncertainty whether the experimental and control groups are indeed equivalent after randomization, and (2) loss of pretreatment base-line data.

For certain programs, the population of interest will itself be a pretested one. For example, Anderson (1975) has noted that participants in a national income maintenance program probably would be required to fill out forms and questionnaires prior to receiving cash transfers, in much the same way as is required of persons participating in the current experiments. In this case, or in similar cases, the use of a pretest-posttest design could enhance the external validity of the experiment since the experimental design is isomorphic with the actual program that might be implemented.

POSTTEST SENSITIZATION

Bracht and Glass (1968) pointed out that the administration of the posttest may interact with the treatment, thereby producing results that would not be observed in a population that received the treatment, but was not posttested. They (1968: 464) argued that:

> treatment effects may be latent or incomplete and appear only when formally posttested in the experimental setting. In the natural setting where post-tests are absent, treatment effects may not appear for a want of a sensitizing post-test.

To illustrate, suppose one is interested in the effectiveness of TV spots in changing attitudes toward hiring the handicapped. Time is bought from randomly chosen TV viewing areas, and a posttest is administered both in areas where the spot was shown and where it was not. It may be that the effects of the spot are latent and incomplete until the respondents are actually asked their attitudes about hiring the handicapped. At this time the asking of the questions and the treatment itself combine to affect the answers provided.

Bracht and Glass suggested that in cases in which the experimenter believes that posttest measurement may itself affect the variable of interest, one should try to employ unobtrusive measures (Webb et al., 1966). However, as Lana (1969) pointed out, the unobtrusive measures available are often unsuitable for many research projects of interest. However, there are some natural experiments in which unobtrusive measures can be meaningfully employed, such as Campbell and Ross's (1968) analysis of the Connecticut crackdown on speeding, and Glass's (1968) analysis of change in Germany's divorce law in 1900. Still, many if not most unobtrusive measures are of unknown reliability and validity.

INTERACTION BETWEEN MEASUREMENT AND INDIVIDUAL LEVEL VARIABLES

Sometimes cognitive and abilities tests measure different variables for certain subgroups of the sample; that is, there is an interaction between measurement and one or more individual level variables. For example, some measures are said not to be "culture free." In the abstract, it is impossible to say whether this is an important threat to external validity, but it is one that the evaluation researcher should consider in choosing measuring instruments. For example, it is clear that questionnaires are inappropriate measuring devices with illiterate or near-illiterate populations, and indeed, any instrument relying on verbal ability including an interview may be problematic. Similarly, the use of the English language with persons not knowing it well leads to equally obvious problems.

The disadvantaged, certain ethnic groups, and very young children do pose special measurement problems for the evaluator. At the same time, some of the arguments raised seem to be political in nature and follow rather than precede the publication of findings, especially negative findings for a popular program that was supposed to have led to some desired change. One of the criticisms leveled at the Westinghouse evaluation of Head Start was the use of instruments not developed for disadvantaged children in measuring cognitive and affective states. But as Williams and Evans (1972) noted, previous studies with these same instruments that showed positive results had rarely been questioned. If nothing more, the potential for such political responses to measures used places emphasis on the need for studies explicitly designed to assess the validity of measures.

OMISSION OF RELEVANT DEPENDENT VARIABLES

One claim sometimes made is that a set of negative findings are "invalid" because the study failed to measure all of the relevant dependent variables. For example, Williams and Evans (1972) related that some critics of the Westinghouse evaluation of Head Start noted that only cognitive and affective variables were measured, and not measures of health, nutrition, and community objectives as well. If the Head Start programs were designed to affect these latter variables, the criticism would have been valid. However, reviews of the Head Start experience suggest that there was no single Head Start program, but instead a set of very different programs which varied from center to center. As several evaluation methodologists have noted (Freeman and Sherwood, 1965; Suchman, 1967; Hyman and Wright, 1967; Bernstein and Sheldon, 1975), adequate evaluation research depends on agreement of clearly specified program goals. Without this agreement (or acknowledgment of a lack of it) prior to executing the research, every evaluation may be invalid in the sense that someone with a vested interest in the program can later claim that the important goals were not measured.

There are two features characteristic of much of evaluation research that bear on this point. First, because evaluation research is often done in a political setting, different interest groups may hold different goals for the program, some of which may conflict with one another, or at least be unrelated to one another. The evaluation researcher who blindly assumes that the goals formally stated by the program director are definitive may be overlooking what others with political power anticipate for the program. Moreover, he/she may be overlooking, as well, the fact that the target population, the staff, and the agency staff funding the action program may also each have a set of goals in mind and not necessarily a set the same as those enunciated by the program administrator. To illustrate: a former high-ranking administrator of OEO once noted that Head Start was largely born out of political motives: OEO believed it would be popular with congressmen and their constituents. This observation is supported by the fact that Head Start has continued in spite of the negative evaluation it received from the Westinghouse Corporation. This suggests that someone's goals were being met, although they most certainly were not those specified and measured in the formal evaluation.

Second, and related to the above, is that the problem of specifying the goals of a particular program is particularly difficult because, unlike most research which begins with a dependent variable, or a set of dependent variables for which causes are sought, much evaluation research begins with an independent variable and asks what it causes. Typically, a social scientist states an interest in some y and asks which set of x's are causally related to it. In evaluation research, one begins with an x (the program) and asks what y's it might affect. One can think of a host of variables that a Head Start program, or a negative income tax program, could affect. As such, it is hard to imagine that a priori all of the dependent variables of potential interest will be specified and measured. Thus, the problem results from the fact that programs often begin with the purpose of helping in some general way, but "how" is left largely undefined yet with implication that the how is self-obvious.

The implication of these two features is that valid inferences about the range of effects, or about all of the effects of a social experiment, are much more difficult to make than are inferences from the typical basic-science experiment, other things being equal. Unlike traditional research where the objectives of the research are specified with great care, the evaluation researcher needs to survey carefully those who will be affected by a program, e.g., administrators, staff, and clients, in order to determine the multiplicity of goals that a single program may be expected to serve.

The above discussion is not meant to suggest that findings associated with only some subset of goals for a program will be totally invalid. Rather, our intention is to point out that the structure of evaluation research often requires the researcher to do a prior study in order not to omit variables which reflect important areas of concern for agencies and groups associated with the program in some significant way.

LACK OF CORRESPONDENCE BETWEEN MEASUREMENT AND CAUSAL LAG

One of the difficulties in any research is knowing in advance how much of a time lag exists between application of a treatment and the manifestation of its effect. The effects might be immediate, or they may occur weeks, months, or even years later. Similarly, the effects may be gradual and continuous, or they may occur all at once. Obviously, if the measurement lag (the time between administration of the treatment and its measurement) does not correspond to the causal lag, the evaluation researcher will arrive at incorrect conclusions about the effects of the independent variables (Pelz and Lew, 1970). Hovland et al. (1949) have discussed the well-known "sleeper effect," in which armed forces personnel predisposed to an idea did not show attitude changes immediately after seeing a film, but did show change nine weeks later. Similarly, Borgatta and Evans (1968) showed that antismoking messages did not have an effect until a follow-up a year after the negative findings had been observed.

One evaluation that attempted to assess immediate, intermediate, and long-range effects of a program was the evaluation of the Encampment for Citizenship Program (Hyman et al., 1962). Using an elaboration of what Campbell and Stanley (1963) called a "patched up" design (see Table 1), this evaluation took measures directly preceding the program and immediately after the program to estimate the *immediate* effects ($0_3 - 0_2$, $0_8 - 0_7$, $0_{12} - 0_{11}$, $0_{16} - 0_{15}$ in Figure 1). To estimate the short-term stability of this effect, they compared $0_4 - 0_3$ to $0_3 - 0_2$, using $0_2 - 0_1$ as an estimate for change which would occur as a result of normal maturation. To estimate the *intermediate* effect of the program, they took measures two months after the campers had returned and compared them with the before-after measures: $0_9 - 0_7$ and $0_8 - 0_7$; $0_{13} - 0_{11}$ and $0_{12} - 0_{11}$; and $0_{17} - 0_{15}$ and $0_{16} - 0_{15}$. Last, to measure *long-range effects,* they obtained after-only measures for camp alumni for a period of nine years, and a four-years-after measure was taken on the original New York 1955 group. The use of the alumni follow-up not only extended the range to nine years after exposure, but also allowed the evaluators to chart any discernible patterns in changes as the time lapse since leaving the encampment program increased. Thus by comparing $0_{26} - 0_{11}$ to $0_{12} - 0_{11}$, $0_{25} - 0_{11}$ to $0_{12} - 0_{11} \ldots 0_{18} - 0_{11}$ to $0_{12} - 0_{11}$ they estimated the long-range effects of the program for the period from one to nine years after the camping experience.

In summation, we have discussed six types of measurement problems which can affect the generalizability of results: (1) measurement error per se, (2) pretest sensitization, (3) posttest sensitization, (4) interaction between measurement and individual level characteristics, (5) omission of relevant dependent variables, and (6) the lack of isomorphism between measurement and causal lags.

CONFOUNDED TREATMENT EFFECTS

In most experiments observational units are randomized into one of the treatment control conditions, and there is no ambiguity about which observational units have received which treatment. Unfortunately, with social experimentation in natural settings it is often difficult to determine what the treatment really is. Some subjects may be participating in several programs, and hence there is no uniform treatment (or set of treatments) for all subjects in a given treatment condition. In still other cases, subjects whose eligibility characteristics have changed (eligibility determines which

TABLE 1
Evaluation of Encampment Programs—An Example of an Elaboration Design

Groups	Before Measures			After Measures			Years After								
	6 weeks Before Program	First Day Of Arrival	Program	Last Day Of Program	6 Wks. After	2 Mo. After	1	2	3	4	5	6	7	8	9
N.Y. 1955	O_1*	O_2	X_1	O_3	O_4	O_9				O_5					
N.Y. 1957	O_6	O_7	X_2	O_8		O_{13}									
N.Y. 1958	O_{10}	O_{11}	X_3	O_{12}		O_{17}									
Cal. 1958**	O_{14}	O_{15}	X_4	O_{16}											
Alumni 1946			X_5													O_{18}
Alumni 1947			X_6												O_{19}	
Alumni 1948			X_7											O_{20}		
Alumni 1949			X_8										O_{21}			
Alumni 1950			X_9									O_{22}				
Alumni 1951			X_{10}								O_{23}					
Alumni 1952			X_{11}							O_{24}						
Alumni 1953			X_{12}						O_{25}							
Alumni 1954			X_{13}					O_{26}								

*Only one-third of the campers were sent a questionnaire six weeks before arriving at the Encampment. This was done in order to obtain a measure of normal maturation over a six week period. Normal maturation then was the difference between $O_2 - O_1$.

**The California 1958 Encampment was added to vary the ecological setting. Whereas in New York (Riverdale) the program was set up like a total community, in California it was less self-contained.

treatment condition they are in) may "wander" from treatment condition to treatment condition throughout the life of the experiment. Finally, there are cases in which treatment effects are apparently specific only to subjects with certain characteristics. All of these effects can be grouped together and termed "confounded treatment effects."

LACK OF STANDARD TREATMENTS ACROSS SAMPLING UNITS

In our earlier discussion of selection of sample units by excellence, we noted that evaluation studies often attempt to assess the effectiveness of multiple programs by observing a sample of them. For example, the Head Start evaluation by Westinghouse examined a sample of 104 Head Start centers in order to assess the effectiveness of the Head Start Program in precipitating intellectual and social-personal development among first-, second-, and third-grade children. However, taking a probability sample of local programs provides no assurance that the programs were alike in terms of implementation. As McDill et al. (1972: 149) discussing Title I programs asserted,

> Most governmental poverty programs have earmarked federal funds to be used in an area of recognized need but have left the determination of the means and goals to be pursued almost entirely to those at the local level. Thus the individual programs "purchased" with these monies and the rationales behind them are diffuse, a point which must always be kept in mind when a national program is evaluated.

These authors noted further the wide variation in emphasis and services provided by the various Head Start projects.

One can conclude from the above that, when national programs are being evaluated, a random sample of local versions of that program provides no basis for generalizability about the effectiveness of a single program. Rather what seems appropriate is a design that carefully specifies in detailed ways program inputs and program outputs, and a list of local projects that share these specific definitions of inputs and outputs. Once that list of projects has been compiled, process measure evaluations should be examined for each, i.e., measures should be taken to assess whether or not the program has been implemented according to stated guidelines. A new list can then be formulated of projects that have indeed implemented the same set of program inputs for the purpose of attaining the same set of desired outputs. From that list, a probability sample can be drawn to assess the effectiveness of programs with components ABC to effect changes XYZ. And those results can be generalizable to other programs with the same inputs. However, this assumes that project centers are randomly assigned to treatments, and further, that differential adherence to program guidelines is random. Selective factors related to the effects of interest may also determine the degree to which the guidelines are followed.

Alternatively, if one knows ex post facto how local projects differ from one another, and if one assumes that these differences are randomly distributed among the projects, then these differences can be treated as a set of treatments and the data analyzed using traditional analysis-of-variance techniques. The problem, of course, is that it probably is incorrect to make the assumption that the various project centers are randomly assigned in fact to the various treatments.

MULTIPLE TREATMENT EFFECTS

Campbell and Stanley (1963: 6) posited that multiple treatment effects are likely to occur when subjects have participated in multiple programs aimed at effecting change. Similarly, Bracht and Glass (1968: 438) asserted that multiple treatment interference precludes generalizations to populations which have not been subjected to the same sequential set of multiple treatments. In evaluation research, this problem is particularly severe since the research is so often aimed at assessing the effectiveness of programs for the socially and economically disadvantaged, a population often comprising persons participating in several social action programs.

In terms of external validity, the problem is generalizing to populations of persons who have or have not participated in multiple programs, and/or separating out the effects of participation in one program from those of having participated in more than one program. For example, persons receiving monies from the Negative Income Tax Experiment may also be participating in Model Cities Programs, Job Training Programs, and the like. The researcher measuring change on any particular variable can never be certain which program should be credited with precipitating the desired change. Also, it may be that participation in a number of programs may involve subtle selective processes on the part of clients disposed to change, or simply the participation in many programs may establish a "culture of change" for the clients.

It remains unclear whether simultaneous participation in multiple programs has selective, additive, or interaction effects. Even if changes are noted, the population for which results are generalizable remains unclear. In order to help assess whether multiple treatments are occurring, clients could be (a) asked to respond to a set of items designed to assess multiple program participation, and (b) asked to report their history of participation in the program being evaluated. Unless one can make the assumption that subjects are randomly distributed among the various multiple treatment effects, there really is no good solution to the problem of generalizability. If, however, the assumption of random assignment seems reasonable, one can apply the analysis of covariance, although this assumes no interaction between the various multiple treatment effects and the experimental program variable(s). Equivalently, one can construct a dummy variable for each presumed multiple treatment effect and test for its significance within a multiple regression framework (Cohen, 1968; Kerlinger and Pedhazur, 1973).

Another variety of multiple treatment effects also can be noted. This one applies to programs that define the treatment condition to which one is assigned according to a set of eligibility criteria. For example, the New Jersey Income Maintenance Program was limited to married, male-headed families in five metropolitan areas in New Jersey and Pennsylvania. However, during the course of the three-year experiment, some experimental families became eligible for AFDC because of the loss of a husband due to death, desertion, divorce, or separation. Such families were required to report all AFDC income to the evaluators, but cash transfers to these families from the experiment were not reduced. Similarly, the Gary income program used criteria based on age, family composition, and income to define eligibility for participation in the program, but changes in these variables meant that the treatment for certain subjects changed with changes in the variables defining eligibility.

Again, if such wandering can be thought of as occurring randomly across treatment conditions, one might code "wanders" as a dummy variable and estimate the seriousness of the bias. The severity of the problem depends, of course, on the prevalence of the condition. If only a small percentage of the subjects change in these ways, the estimates of treatment effects will be only minimally affected. On the other hand, if this "movement" is considerable, one must question whether a set of discrete treatments existed at all.

INTERACTION OF INDIVIDUAL LEVEL VARIABLES
WITH THE EXPERIMENTAL TREATMENT EFFECTS

When there are interactions between the treatment and the individual level variables, generalizability of inferences may be severely limited. Lubin (1961) noted two classes of interaction effects. In one case a treatment has opposite effects for different classes of persons (called disordinal interaction); in the other, the effects are in the same direction (ordinal interaction). Knowing that ordinal interaction exists is of importance since it suggests that the cost-benefit ratio differs for different subgroups of the sample. However, the problems for inference when disordinal interaction exists are patently more serious. Few published examples of disordinal interaction can be located, suggesting that it may be a relatively rare problem. Another possibility is that few researchers check for it. One exception is the work of Hunt and Hardt (1969) who, in a study of disadvantaged high school students, found that over a 21-month period the GPAs of the black Upward Bound students and their controls both decreased while the white students in both the experimental and control groups increased, although the increase was not significant.

While the number of individual level variables that might interact with a treatment is very large, it seems imperative that the evaluator at least consider as possibilities some standard sociological variables such as age, sex, race, education, and income. The last three virtually define what we mean by "disadvantaged." Since many social action programs are directed at the disadvantaged, one would want to be certain that at least these variables are not interacting with the treatment in a way which suggests that the treatment is effective only for the more "advantaged" in the sample.

In summation, we have reviewed three types of confounded treatment effects which might affect generalizability: (1) the lack of a single treatment across sampling units, (2) multiple treatment effects, and (3) the interaction of individual level variables with the experimental treatment. In the final section which follows, we treat a broad class of threats to external validity termed situational effects.

SITUATIONAL EFFECTS[1]

Threats to external validity may be posed by the fact that the experiment, be it natural or contrived, occurs in a particular context not representative of all contexts to which one wishes to generalize. Hyman and Wright (1967), discussing evaluation research methods, suggested that one take care to consider the effects of the ecology, setting, and staff of social program experiments since it is not unlikely that these factors will interact in some significant ways with the treatment effects. The following represent factors which seem most likely to be problematic for the external validity of evaluation research studies.

STAFF EFFECTS

Evaluation researchers have long since recognized that observed effects may be dependent on the administrator, director, group leader, or therapist directly involved with program administration. To illustrate, the effectiveness of a therapy program for soon-to-be-released convicts may depend heavily on the charismatic abilities of the therapist(s), rather than on a particular therapeutic approach. Unless the personal qualities of the staff are treated as part of the specific program input, and findings are noted to be generalizable only to programs administered by staff with equivalent personal qualities, the results cannot be generalizable.

It is this "situational factor" that may account for the difficulty often noted in implementing a successful widespread effort based on an earlier successful demonstration program. That is, uniqueness may be associated with the effort of a staff that believes in the effectiveness of the program. However, the same ability, ideological commitment, and enthusiasm may not be present among those involved in a later effort for widespread implementation of the program. Cain and Hollister (1972: 117) made a similar point in stating that to focus on the characteristics of the staff may be to focus on the nonreplicable aspects of the program: "it has sometimes been stated that the success of a compensatory education program depended upon the warmth and enthusiasm of the teachers. In a context of a nationwide program, [however] no administrator has control over the level of warmth and enthusiasm of teachers."

Apart from the action program staff, the evaluation staff may pose a problem, although it is less likely since presumably they have no stake in either positive or negative results regarding program effectiveness. However, in some instances, it may be that the presence of the evaluator may create a particular environment, e.g., the staff may feel threatened by him/her, or the clients may be aware of the evaluators which may then affect the clients' behavior. This latter point is treated more fully in the next section.

Staff effects such as the above may be seen as analogous to the so-called "experimenter effects" that are treated in great detail in the social psychological literature of the past several years, e.g., McGuire (1969) and Rosenthal (1969).

HAWTHORNE EFFECTS

The Hawthorne effect refers to changes in the attitudes or behaviors of subjects in an experiment precipitated by the awareness of being observed. Most often the Hawthorne effect results in an increased effort on the part of the subject to try to do that which he/she perceives as desirous or socially acceptable, although the client can just as well try to perform badly if so motivated. The first case in which this effect was noted involved a study of factory workers in the Western Electric Company. The workers responded favorably to almost all experimental changes in the work environment, such as lighting and music. Roethlisberger and Dickson (1939) eventually concluded that their observation of an increased work effort could not be attributed to changes in light intensity or to the addition of music, since responses to these innovations were being confounded by the subjects' awareness of the experiment.

In evaluation research settings, knowledge of being a participant in an evaluation of an experimental program can produce similarly biased effects. This can be especially problematic if program participants recognize that the results of the evaluation may be used in the decision process which determines the fate of the experimental program. Moreover, it is sometimes reported that staff with a vested interest in the continuance of the program may play on this known reaction to experimental evaluation. That is, staff may use as the basis for "pep talks" and encouragement for increased effort such statements as, "Our group is being observed as an important experimental group and therefore, we should do our best to be the very best ever . . . such that in the future everyone can have. . . ." The problem is that the findings must be generalizable to other settings in which the experimental nature of the program may no longer be a factor. The question one is left with, then, is whether the same effects would occur in a nonexperimental setting where the participants are not being evaluated. However, one must not overestimate these effects either, since in the absence of an experiment the staff might still give such "pep talks" for equally important reasons, e.g., to get ahead themselves, because they do want to help the clients, or even to keep the program alive. In fact, one might argue that such factors should be incorporated into every program if indeed they are found to function to persuade the client to perform in a way that results in desired behavioral or status changes.

Working on the identical problem, social psychologists have attempted various procedures aimed at ruling out the biases posed by "demand characteristics," demand characteristics being the effects of the subject's perception of his or her role in the experiment and/or his or her perception of the hypothesis being tested. Orne (1969: 144-145) stated:

> Because subjects are active, sentient beings, they do not respond to the specific experimental stimuli with which they are confronted as isolated events but rather they perceive these in the total context of the experimental situation. . . . The subject's recognition that he is not merely responding to a set of stimuli but is doing so in order to produce data may exert an influence upon his performance. Inevitably he will wish to produce "good" data, that is, data characteristic of a "good" subject.

Unlike experimenter effects, which can be studied and somewhat controlled for by varying experimenters, demand characteristics are not so easily uncovered, since demand characteristic effects depend partly on the subject's perception. Orne (1969) suggested three methods for dealing with demand characteristics; only the first is applicable for evaluation research. The first method is what he terms "postexperimental inquiry," i.e., inquiring into the subject's perception of the experiment's demand characteristics after it is completed. While this seems useful, importantly it does not eliminate the bias, but rather serves to document whether or not it is a problem worthy of concern. It is useful for evaluation research if one discovers that the perception of certain demand characteristics increases the likelihood of change in the desired direction. Given the purpose is always to discover some effective method of inducing desired change, the explication of demand characteristics can become a deliberate part of program inputs for future implementations.

NOVELTY EFFECTS

Bracht and Glass (1968) defined "novelty effects" as that which occurs when some new treatment is first introduced. In evaluation settings, the newness of the program may precipitate a response to the treatment that would not occur under more ordinary conditions. The possibility of this novelty effect further demonstrates the need for measures of the stability of effects over time. Previously, we referenced the patched-up design as used by Hyman et al. (1962). It would seem that a design that provides comparative estimates of effects on replicated instances of the same program would be useful as a mechanism for reducing errors of inference posed by the bias of novelty effects. For example, if the effects attributed to the implementation of the encampment program were far greater in the first year (New York 1955) than in later years (New York 1957), then one could conclude that novelty effects, the effects of the newness of the program, were interacting with the treatment outcomes. Replication thus seems to be one useful way of controlling for novelty effects.

HISTORY

Just as the experimental setting may affect the outcome of the treatment program, so the historical time in which an experiment takes place may also affect the outcome of the treatment program. Many of the experimental social action programs recently evaluated were conceived and implemented during the late sixties, a historical period that clearly could not be characterized as typical.[2] It is not hard to imagine that the emotion-packed, liberation-reform tempo of that period probably affected the attitudes and behaviors of the socially and economically disadvantaged. And this might well have affected the way in which the disadvantaged population responded to program treatments aimed at social reform and social rehabilitation. The problem now is for decision makers to draw inferences from these evaluations and to generalize from them for the purpose of policy decisions about programs that will be implemented and executed in times not characterized by such political and social upheaval in, say, the quite different recession period of the 1970s.

One way of dealing with the threat posed to external validity by the interaction of history with treatment effects is to replicate the experimental treatment at various points in time. Since replication also helps to eliminate other threats to external validity we underscore its value. Bernstein and Freeman (1975: ch. 7), in setting forth a set of policy recommendations for evaluation research, suggested that experimental programs be implemented and evaluated long before relevant policy decisions need to be made. Such long-range preplanning would allow for replications over time of the experimental program in varied settings with varied staff and varied program inputs. Done this way, the culminating experimental program could be a program based on modifications made in accordance with systematic, ongoing evaluation. Furthermore, such a procedure would increase the likelihood of program effectiveness and would allow for some control over sampling fluctuations, setting, history, and/or staff interactions with the treatment effects. However, this requires a willingness to commit funds for experimental program ressearch that, with only a few exceptions, is not characteristic of government policy thus far. The more common policy has been to try a program only after the need for it has become acute and thus long after the time for repeated experimentation has passed.

GEOGRAPHIC SETTING

> In the attempt to conceptualize a program, the evaluator may be led astray by the very term itself. He may think of the treatment and forget the context in which it is imbedded.... [Importantly] the staff and the program are contained within a site, and the ecology of sites often contributes to the effectiveness of programs and should [thus] be conceptualized by an evaluator [Hyman and Wright, 1967: 196].

The geographic site in which an experimental program takes place might well interact with the treatment to produce particular outcomes that might not occur were the program set in alternate sites. For example, in some programs subjects are removed from their natural environment and taken for treatment to an environment better suited to the execution of the treatment. The Daytop Village Drug Rehabilitation Program is a case in point. Hard core drug addicts from the New York metropolitan area were taken to a country estate overlooking Long Island Sound, where they lived for several years in a commune-type arrangement and participated in a self-examination, self-help therapy program. The program directors asserted that the core of the program was the self-examination, self-help therapy sessions. However, when a similar program was instituted in a tenement in New York's lower east side, program administrators soon realized that the country setting, because of its aesthetic pleasantness and/or lack of access to drugs, was an important component of the rehabilitation program. Apparently, they had made an error in generalizing the experience of the country setting site to similar programs set in different sites.

A similar finding was noted by Hyman et al. (1962) in their evaluation of the encampment program. By comparing the observations of participants in the New York program (located in an isolated residential site) with observations of participants in the California program (located in a large major city), they detected what appeared to be interaction effects between the ecology of the setting and the encampment program. Campers in the New York program showed more marked changes on the desired outcome variables than did campers in the comparable California program. In both the Daytop experiment and the encampment experiment, geographic setting was suggested post hoc as the crucial variable accounting for the observed differences. However, in fact, differences may have been due to staff, procedural, or other factors. Once again, replicating the experimental program over varied geographical settings would help to sort out the effects of experimental sites.

EFFECTS DUE TO DIFFERENTIAL MORTALITY

Differential mortality effects stem from differential subject and program losses from social experiments. If the loss of observational units is different for the treatment and control groups, and the differences cannot be attributed to chance, then external validity is threatened. While estimation models exist for missing data when the attrition is assumed to be random across treatment and control conditions, they do not appear to be models applicable when the sample loss is assumed to be nonrandom. Unfortunately, it is the latter case, where attrition cannot be assumed to be nonrandom, that may be typical of much evaluation research.

DIFFERENTIAL ATTRITION OF SUBJECTS

In experiments involving desired services such as income maintenance, nutrition supplements, and the like, it is realistic to assume that differential attrition will occur between the experimental and the control conditions since the motivation to continue in the study is significantly lower for the control subjects. For example, Kershaw (1972) indicated that in the income maintenance experiments attrition indeed was higher in the control group than in the experimental groups, even though counterattrition methods were employed.

Minimally, it seems that evaluators need to determine what the correlates of differential attrition are in order to further the development of new counterattrition methods. Presently, the personnel of the Gary Income Maintenance Experiment are considering a simulation experiment to determine the effects of differential attrition on the estimates of interest. This appears to be a reasonable way to proceed; hopefully, their efforts will provide useful suggestions.

DIFFERENTIAL ATTRITION OF PROGRAMS

Generally, when one thinks of threats to validity posed by differential mortality, the reference is to attrition of subjects in an experimental situation. Because of the political nature of evaluation research, the attrition problem is often more complex insofar as the attrition may not only be of subjects, but of whole programs as well. For example, if a national evaluation of "X" poverty program is being conducted and a random sample is taken of local X poverty programs for the evaluation study, when local programs drop out of the sample because they have been canceled (for whatever reason) the external validity of the findings can be called into question. This is especially problematic if it is the case that canceled programs were characterized by a blatant lack of effectiveness, corruption, or the like. Thus, unless one can assume that sample mortality is randomly distributed, generalizability is limited.

CONCLUSION

Our purpose here has been to provide a codification and discussion of factors that preclude maximum utility of evaluation research findings by virtue of the limits they place on generalizability. As threats to external validity, these factors potentially stand in the way of policy makers, who need to draw inferences from individual studies so as to be able to decide rationally whether programs should be modified, terminated, or expanded. This list should be most useful to evaluation researchers as a checklist against which precautions should be taken in designing and executing evaluation studies.

Suggestions have been put forth to rule out some of the biases noted. However, not all of the suggestions will always be feasible nor have suggestions been provided for all of the potential threats. Our hope is that this illumination of factors will aid future efforts in experimentation with methods and models that control for threats to external validity. And that in so doing, the state of evaluation research methodology will be advanced.

NOTES

1. Bracht and Glass (1968) include many of the same factors as falling under the rubric of "ecological validity."

2. Of course, one can easily argue that no period is "typical."

REFERENCES

ANDERSON, A. (1975) Principal Investigator: Evaluation of Gary Income Maintenance Experiment. Personal conversations with author.

BERNSTEIN, I. and H. E. FREEMAN (1975) Academic and Entrepreneurial Research: The Consequences of Diversity in Federal Evaluation Studies. New York: Russell Sage.

BERNSTEIN, I. and E. B. SHELDON (1975) "Method of evaluative research," in R. Smith (ed.) Social Science Methods. New York: Free Press.

BORGATTA, E. F. and R. R. EVANS (1968) Smoking and Health. Chicago: Aldine.

BRACHT, G. H. and G. V. GLASS (1968) "The external validity of experiments." Amer. Educ. Research J. 5: 437-474.

CAIN, G. C. and R. G. HOLLISTER (1972) "The methodology of evaluating social action programs," pp. 109-137 in P. Rossi and W. Williams (eds.) Evaluating Social Programs. New York: Seminar Press.

CAMPBELL, D. T. (1969) "Perspective: artifact and control," pp. 351-382 in R. Rosenthal and R. L. Rosnow (eds.) Artifact in Behavioral Research. New York: Academic Press.

——— (1957) "Factors relevant to the validity of experiments in social settings." Psych. Bull. 54: 297-312.

——— and H. L. ROSS (1968) "The Connecticut crackdown in speeding: time-series data in quasi experimental analysis." Law and Society Rev. 3, 1: 33-53.

CAMPBELL, D. and J. C. STANLEY (1963) Experimental and Quasi-Experimental Designs for Research. Chicago: Rand McNally.

COHEN, J. (1968) "Multiple regression as a general data analytic system." Psych. Bull. 70: 426-443.

CORNFIELD, J. and J. W. TUKEY (1956) "Average values of mean squares in factorials." Annals of Mathematical Statistics 27: 907-949.

FREEMAN, H. E. and C. C. SHERWOOD (1965) "Research in large-scale intervention programs," pp. 262-276 in F. G. Caro (ed.) Readings in Evaluation Research. New York: Russell Sage.

GLASS, G. V. (1968) "Analysis of data on the Connecticut speeding crackdown as a time series quasi-experiment." Law and Society Rev. 3, 1: 55-76.

HOVLAND, C. I., A. A. LUMSDAINE, and F. D. SHEFFIELD (1949) Experiments on Mass Communication. Princeton: Princeton Univ. Press.

HUNT, D. E. and R. H. HARDT (1969) "The effect of Upward Bound programs on the attitudes, motivation, and academic achievement of Negro students." J. of Social Times 25: 117-129.

HYMAN, H. and C. R. WRIGHT (1967) "Evaluating social action programs," pp. 185-220 in F. G. Caro (ed.) Readings in Evaluation Research. New York: Russell Sage.

——— and T. HOPKINS (1962) Applications of Methods of Evaluation: Four Studies of the Encampment for Citizenship. Berkeley: Univ. of California Press.

KERLINGER, F. N. and E. J. PEDHAZUR (1973) Multiple Regression in Behavioral Research. New York: Holt, Rinehart & Winston.

KERSHAW, D. (1972) "Issues in income maintenance experimentation," in P. H. Rossi and W. Williams (eds.) Evaluating Social Programs. New York: Seminar Press.

LANA, R. E. (1969) "Pretest sensitization," pp. 119-141 in R. Rosenthal and R. L. Rosnow (eds.) Artifact in Behavioral Research. New York: Academic Press.

LORD, F. N. and M. R. NOVICK (1968) Statistical Theories of Mental Test Scores. Reading, Mass.: Addison-Wesley.

LUBIN, A. (1961) "The interpretation of significant interaction." Educ. and Psych. Measurement 21: 807-817.

McDILL, E. L., M. S. McDILL, and J. T. SPREHE (1972) "Evaluation in practice: contemporary education," pp. 141-185 in P. Rossi and W. Williams (eds.) Evaluating Social Programs. New York: Seminar Press.

McGUIRE, W. J. (1969) "Suspiciousness of experimenter 'intent', " pp. 13-57 in R. Rosenthal and R. L. Rosnow (eds.) Artifact in Behavioral Research. New York: Academic Press.

ORNE, M. T. (1969) "Demand characteristics and the concept of quasi controls," pp. 143-179 in R. Rosenthal and R. L. Rosnow (eds.) Artifact in Behavioral Research. New York: Academic Press.

PELZ, D. C. and R. A. LEW (1970) "Heise's causal model applied," pp. 28-37 in E. F. Borgatta and G. W. Bohrnstedt (eds.) Sociological Methodology. San Francisco: Jossey-Bass.

ROETHLISBERGER, K. and W. DICKSON (1939) Management and the Worker. Cambridge: Harvard Univ. Press.

ROSENBERG, M. J. (1969) "The conditions and consequences of evaluation apprehension," pp. 279-349 in R. Rosenthal and R. L. Rosnow (eds.) Artifact in Behavioral Research. New York: Academic Press.

ROSENTHAL, R. (1969) "Interpersonal expectations: effects of the experimenter 'o hypothesis," pp. 181-277 in R. Rosenthal and R. L. Rosnow (eds.) Artifact in Behavioral Research. New York: Academic Press.

ROSSI, P. (1972) "Testing for success and failure in social action," pp. 11-49 in P. Rossi and W. Williams (eds.) Evaluating Social Programs. New York: Seminar Press.

――― and W. WILLIAMS [eds.] (1972) Evaluating Social Programs. New York: Seminar Press.

SUCHMAN, E. (1967) Evaluative Research. New York: Russell Sage.

WEBB, E. J. et al. (1966) Unobtrusive Measures: Nonreactive Research in the Social Sciences. Chicago: Rand McNally.

WEISS, C. (1970) "The politicization of evaluation research." J. of Social Issues 26, 4: 57-67.

WILLIAMS, W. and J. W. EVANS (1972) "The politics of evaluation: the case of Head Start," pp. 247-264 in P. Rossi and W. Williams (eds.) Evaluating Social Programs. New York: Seminar Press.